Cat Lover's Devotional

Print ISBN 978-1-61626-829-9

eBook Editions:
Adobe Digital Edition (.epub) 978-1-62029-072-9
Kindle and MobiPocket Edition (.prc) 978-1-62029-073-6

Published by Barbour Publishing, Inc., P.O. Box 719, Uhrichsville, Ohio 44683,
www.barbourbooks.com

*Our mission is to publish and distribute inspirational products offering exceptional value
and biblical encouragement to the masses.*

Member of the
Evangelical Christian
Publishers Association

Printed in the United States of America.

Cat Lover's Devotional

What We Learn about Life from Our Feline Friends

Katherine A. Douglas

BARBOUR
PUBLISHING

Dedication

*This book is lovingly dedicated
to my "other" parents,
Don and Harriet Douglas*

Acknowledgments

From friends living in such faraway places as Burkina Faso, Africa, to my nieces two miles up the road, I've garnered the stories you will read in this collection. Once again my gracious mother was my tireless first editor. Mark, my husband, coach, and encourager, would give me hours of solitude, telling people the truth: "She's at work. May I take a message?" My personal delight in this book has been the hours upon hours I've spent in the Word of God. Lessons taught us by cats parallel biblical truth. It has been marvelously gratifying to learn in a new light the admonition of Psalm 150:6: "Let everything that has breath praise the LORD."

Thanks to all of you who have given me such edifying, poignant, instructional, and humorous stories to include in this book.

Contents

Preface

*B*ut ask the animals, and they will teach you" (Job 12:7).

From the oldest book of the Bible we are instructed to learn from the animals. Cats are known for their speed, strength, and stealth. We may be intrigued by a tiny, fearless kitten who climbs to dizzying heights, or we may stare openmouthed before the television at the powerful muscles of a tiger as he races across open country. From the extremes of a mewing, eyes-yet-unopened kitten to the roaring king of the jungle, cats are a unique kind of animal.

As people, we love 'em or hate 'em with scarcely anyone falling somewhere in the middle.

Cat lovers enjoy domestic cats for a variety of reasons. They are entertaining. They are independent. They have beautiful eyes and silky soft fur. They are fastidiously clean but don't mind getting dirty if they're intent on a task. They are smart, curious, resourceful, and amazingly resilient. Cats are persistent hunters—and shameless loungers.

In this collection of true stories, you'll see a number of lessons taught by our feline friends. Cats demonstrate adaptability. They model uncommon perseverance and steadfastness. They show us character qualities that God wants us to put off—anger, brawling, arrogance (Ephesians 4:25–31; Romans 11:20). Conversely, our cats may teach us lessons in self-control, service, or. . . relaxation techniques. We need only be teachable to garner some invaluable lessons from these delightfully unpredictable creatures.

One of the titles of the Lord Jesus Christ is the triumphant "Lion of the tribe of Judah" (Revelation 5:5). We can emulate Him, this Lion of Judah. We're told that "the righteous are as bold as a lion" (Proverbs 28:1) and that to be brave is to have "the heart of a lion" (2 Samuel 17:10). Cats aren't just stealth, strength, and speed.

Delight in the truth that "in [God's] hand is the life of every creature and the breath of all mankind" (Job 12:10). Today share a smile with another cat lover as you squeeze a "cat nip" between running errands and cleaning the litter box.

Kathy Douglas

God: His Person. . . His Ways

The smallest feline is a masterpiece.

LEONARDO DA VINCI

Pouncer

David took up this lament concerning
Saul and his son Jonathan: . . .
"In life they were loved and admired."

2 SAMUEL 1:17, 23

$\mathcal{F}$ully grown but long, lean, and limber, Pouncer is an unusual cat. He loves violin music. When Caleb, his owner, starts his violin lesson, Pouncer is there to climb up Caleb's leg. He doesn't miss a note. He is enthralled by the notes that pour forth from Caleb's instrument. Unlike most cats, Pouncer also enjoys being groomed. He's even been known to do a complete 360 in midair. Grooming for Pouncer is an event to relish. Above all, Pouncer is a people cat. He loves everybody. He sidles up to family members and total strangers alike. If you're a person, Pouncer takes an immediate liking to you.

If you're a person. But other animals?

There is not an animal on the face of the earth that Pouncer has yet to meet and like. Other cats, dogs, birds, squirrels. . .you name it, and Pouncer doesn't like it. He's been known to tackle a hungry possum head-on. (He came out looking the loser, but the possum was gone in short order.) Once, Pouncer attacked a Rottweiler. (Sometimes Pouncer doesn't show a lot of good sense, but you can't fault him his zeal.) Pouncer is fiercely protective of his domain from the infringement of any other critters. Caleb is at a loss to explain this dual nature of his pet, who is love itself when it comes to people but becomes a vicious attack cat when a "nonperson" is in sight.

David's lament for his dearest friend, Jonathan, is understandable. Throughout the book of 1 Samuel we learn of the deep bond these two men had with one another. Later in David's lament he says: "I grieve for you, Jonathan my brother; you were very dear to me. Your love for me was wonderful, more wonderful than that of women" (2 Samuel 1:26).

David's love for Saul, however, is not so understandable. Throughout his life Saul was either loving David passionately or trying to pin him to the wall (literally) with his spear. David never knew from one day to the next if Saul was going to call him his son or his enemy. Saul was two different men in his dealings with David.

Some of us may have a friend or relative who is like Saul to us. Loving, supportive, and dependable one day, but cross, demanding, and mean spirited the next. Unhappy with themselves, they act out their misery often by hurting those they claim to love. In a word, they make our lives miserable.

The Lord God is never vacillating in His love and

concern for us. He "does not change like shifting shadows" (James 1:17). He is the God who declares: "I have loved you with an everlasting love" (Jeremiah 31:3). We can rest in the unchanging and unchangeable love of God. No matter what comes our way today, He remains the One who "so loved the world that he gave his one and only Son" (John 3:16).

> **The Lord God is never vacillating in His love and concern for us.**

Kit

*The Lord Jesus Christ. . .gave himself for our sins
to rescue us from the present evil age.*

GALATIANS 1:3–4

When she gets hungry, she'll come down."

If Walt had heard those seven words once, he had heard them a hundred times. His cat, Kit, had gotten out of the house undetected. He found her the next morning. Kit had gotten herself up a tree—way up a tree. She lay precariously on a dead branch that jutted out from a towering oak. Like most people, Walt told himself, *When she gets hungry, she'll come down.* After a day or so, however, Kit hadn't moved from her position.

Walt called a tree service. "We don't do animal rescue. When she gets hungry, she'll come down."

Walt called the fire department. "We don't do cats. When she gets hungry, she'll come down."

He tried a number of different sources, but he got the same response. "When she gets hungry, she'll come down."

He tried the fire department one more time. Begrudgingly, they came. The ladder truck was parked under the giant oak and up, up, up went the ladder. At full extension, the fifty-foot ladder was too short. Kit was about seventy-five feet up. They told Walt of another engine house that housed a hundred-foot-ladder truck. He might try them.

Walt called. Same response: "We don't do animal rescue. When she gets hungry, she'll come down."

A week passed. Kit had not moved. Walt tried putting food at the base of the tree; he tried other rescue services. All to no avail. Buzzards had started circling the tree during the day. Desperate, he again called the engine company with the hundred-foot-ladder truck.

"She's still up there?"

The firefighters had a drill that day but said they would stop on their way back to the engine house. Finally, the truck came. The ladder reached. Kit was rescued but not without a fight. It wasn't that Kit wouldn't come down—she couldn't. She had a gaping wound, no doubt from a fight with a raccoon or some other animal.

After some food, water, and a trip to the vet, Kit was as good as new. But she never went any farther than her own backyard again.

Some of us come to our rescuing Savior with tears of joy. A woman who had "lived a sinful life" came to Jesus, finding forgiveness, love, peace, and a fresh start in life (Luke 7:37–50).

Some, like the repentant thief on the cross, come to

Him initially reluctant. They're "out on a limb" like Kit and know they are without recourse. The repentant thief next to Jesus changed his taunts to a plea. "Jesus, remember me when you come into your kingdom" (see Matthew 27:44; Luke 23:42). The disciple Nathanael was initially skeptical of Philip's assessment of Jesus of Nazareth. "Nazareth!" he retorted. "Can anything good come from there?" (John 1:46).

> Whether we come eagerly or dubiously, the Lord kindly and tenderly rescues us.

Whether we come eagerly or dubiously, the Lord kindly and tenderly rescues us. Like the firefighter saving Kit from the circling buzzards, "Jesus. . .rescues us from the coming wrath" (1 Thessalonians 1:10).

Blondie

*They [our fathers] disciplined us for a little while
as they thought best; but God disciplines us for our good,
in order that we may share in his holiness.*

HEBREWS 12:10

*A*hhhh. Motherhood.

Blondie watched her litter of five kittens from her perch on the back of the sofa. It was her first litter. How proud she was! Her brood was so entertaining! Roughhousing and tumbling about in happy play, falling over one another, sneaking up on one another. . . Her kittens were reveling in their playful romp. One of the males began navigating his way up to his mother.

Look at that! Pride swelled her mother's heart. *He's going to try to get up here!*

Blondie stretched and jumped down onto the sofa seat, awaiting her son's ascent. With determination exceeding his size, the little puffball made his way up to his mother. He scampered over to her, his supply of energy seemingly endless.

Reaching his mother, Junior swiped at her face. As tiny as his paw was, his extended claws still hurt. He scratched his mother's eye.

Startled, Blondie paused for only a second or two. Then. . .

Whomp! Whomp! Whomp! Whomp! Whomp!

Blondie boxed her kitten's ears with her padded paw. Without extending her own claws, Blondie gently but firmly swatted the little upstart repeatedly.

Chastised, but no worse for his punishment, Junior went back to play with his siblings. Blondie lay back down.

Ach. Motherhood.

"Know then in your heart that as a man disciplines his son, so the LORD your God disciplines you" (Deuteronomy 8:5). None of us likes to read about the necessity of discipline from the hand of God. Although we laud the parent who lovingly, consistently disciplines her child, when it comes to God disciplining us, we hope for another solution. Yet God is resolute in His desire to fashion us like His Son. His correction is invariably appropriate, timely, and for our good.

> **Our discipline from God is proof of His love—of His fatherhood.**

"My son, do not despise the LORD's discipline, and do not resent his rebuke, because the LORD disciplines those he loves, as a father the son he delights in" (Proverbs 3:11–12; see also Hebrews 12:5–6). Our discipline from God is proof of His love—of His fatherhood. "Endure hardship as discipline," we're told. "God is treating you as his children.

For what children are not disciplined by their father?" (Hebrews 12:7). The writer of Hebrews goes on to say that God's discipline "produces a harvest of righteousness and peace for those who have been trained by it" (verse 11). Experience rings in the words just preceding those words. "No discipline seems pleasant at the time, but painful" (verse 11).

When we feel the sting of God's correction, we can thank Him that His punishment comes from a heart of love. God's discipline is never destructive or inappropriate. "We are being disciplined so that we will not be finally condemned with the world" (1 Corinthians 11:32).

Even if we strike out against the Lord as Junior did with Blondie, we can know that God's "correction and instruction are the way to life" (Proverbs 6:23).

Dude

*D*ude, not one to get his water from some old bowl of water set out on the floor for him, likes his water fresh—right out of the tap. Consequently, Dude would jump into the bathtub to slurp the water that dripped tantalizingly slowly from the bathtub faucet. He would stick out his scratchy pink tongue and relish each transparent drop. It was better than water out of a bowl—or rainwater from a puddle in the street—anytime. Like us, Dude enjoys a drink of fresh water.

Or, rather, he *did* enjoy it.

Not long ago, Dude's owner, Brittany, ran the water into the tub in anticipation of a bath. She turned the water off to go and get one more thing. Dude casually bounded up the stairs from the first floor of the house. He was going to take his afternoon nap upstairs. He stopped before reaching the bedroom.

Why not get a fresh drink first?

Before Brittany could stop or warn him, Dude had sprung up and over the edge of the bathtub.

Dude was all soaking wet black fur, scrambling four feet, and eyes the size of Texas as he leaped from the water-filled tub.

Who had filled up his favorite watering spot with. . . water?

But that wasn't the worst of it.

In his frenzied flight, Dude escaped by jumping on the edge of the toilet. His wet feet couldn't grip the seat. Down he went for a second dousing.

Dude has been drinking from a water bowl on the floor—or a puddle in the street—ever since.

Do you feel some days like you've jumped "from the frying pan into the fire"? Perhaps you've found yourself in a muddle not unlike Dude's. You leaped from one bad situation only to land in the middle of another.

Yesterday you had a bad job. Today you have no job at all. An extended family member misunderstood your attempts to ease some of her debt. She hasn't spoken to you in a month. Your toe isn't bruised; it's broken. Your new cat isn't a fat Henry; she's a pregnant Henrietta. You stopped to smell the roses and got stung by a bee. Sometimes we exit the frying pan and land in the flames.

When three young Hebrew men were thrown into the furnace of fire, the Lord was with them (Daniel 3:16–27).

Immanuel, one of the titles given to the Lord Jesus Christ, means "God with us" (Matthew 1:23). The Lord may not rescue us from the fire, but He won't remain in the skillet when we jump into the fire. (He won't leave the kitchen, either.) "And surely I am with you always," the Lord said, "to the very end of the age" (Matthew 28:20).

> Our God is for us; our God is with us—wherever we find ourselves.

Our God is for us; our God is with us—wherever we find ourselves.

Fudge

You have searched me, LORD, and you know me.
You know when I sit and when I rise;
you perceive my thoughts from afar.

PSALM 139:1–2

He's a pest!

This thought dominates Libby's thinking daily. Libby, a black Labrador, shares the household with Fudge, a black cat who will do anything to get her attention. Fudge loves to play with Libby, but Libby works at avoiding Fudge. Fudge lies in wait for Libby to walk by and then grabs her tail or wraps herself around one of Libby's legs. Libby does her best to ignore Fudge, but Fudge will not be put off.

John and his family try to help Fudge cajole Libby into playing.

"Get kitty! Get kitty!" one of them will command Libby. Yet Fudge sits ignored. He cannot get so much as a glance from his canine companion.

On rare occasions, Fudge gets what he wants. He will plan his attack at just the right moment, catch Libby off guard, and spring on his unsuspecting prey. Startled,

Libby turns on Fudge and growls menacingly.

That solitary growl makes Fudge's day.

"What is man that You have a mind full of him?"

That's how one man paraphrased Psalm 8:4. David penned it this way: "When I consider your heavens, the work of your fingers, the moon and the stars, which you have set in place, what is mankind that you are mindful of them?" (Psalm 8:3–4).

There are no hoops we must jump through or games we must play to be the focus of God's attention. All of Psalm 139 is a declaration of God's constant awareness of each of us. God knows the smallest details about us: He knows when we go out and when we lie down (verse 3). He knows all our idiosyncrasies and habits: "You are familiar with all my ways" (verse 3). This great God also knows the intricacies that make each of us unique and unlike anyone else. "You perceive my thoughts from afar," David wrote. "You created my inmost being" (verses 2, 13).

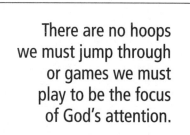

There are no hoops we must jump through or games we must play to be the focus of God's attention.

" 'Who can hide in secret places so that I cannot see them?' declares the LORD. 'Do not I fill heaven and earth?' " (Jeremiah 23:24). God is constantly aware of us—not to spring on us as Fudge does Libby, but because He is

God: everywhere, every*when*, always lovingly conscious of every living being He has made. We don't have to concern ourselves with even the remotest possibility that God is unaware of us, or that He has forgotten us. "Can a mother forget the baby at her breast and have no compassion on the child she has borne?" God asks. He then answers His own question. "Though she may forget, I will not forget you! See, I have engraved you on the palms of my hands" (Isaiah 49:15–16).

Every person you see (or don't see) today matters to God. You matter to God. We have His full attention every second of every hour of every day—whether we want it or not.

Fern, Shocka, and Oreo

In love he predestined us for adoption to sonship through Jesus Christ, in accordance with his pleasure and will.

EPHESIANS 1:4–5

Her niggling suspicion proved true. No good home for the beautiful kittens had been found. They had been taken to the local humane society to await adoption. . .or euthanasia, whichever came first.

Shocka, a regal white cat with some tan coloring splashed in for distinction; Oreo, Shocka's small black-and-white sister; and their colorful calico sister, Fern, were homeless. Their owners were moving and had no place for the new kittens. Neither did they have any takers. The neighbors borrowed Jean's cat carriers under the pretense of having found homes for the fluffy bunch, and the kittens left the neighborhood just before their owners did.

When Jean followed her own instincts and found the left-behind kittens at the pound, she left them there—but she was left in a quandary herself. What if no one adopted them?

She waited until the last hour of the last day before the

kittens' termination. Jean had hoped someone would see the beautiful, personable cats and give them good homes. But "someone" never materialized. Jean took all three cats home.

God gave her, she says, what she neither expected nor prayed about. Her adopted trio has been giving her delight upon delight ever since.

Amy and Keith have no biological children of their own but have adopted a son and daughter from overseas. Clint and Cindy have two children of their own, but they also adopted a neglected child from another country. Ron and Sandi adopted her nephew, whose unstable home situation was untenable.

Adoption is such a beautiful, "flesh and blood" way to demonstrate love. Sometimes the adopted one is beautiful and healthy—like Jean's small litter. Sometimes people adopt children who are less than physically perfect or who are unable to requite their love. These parents lavish love on the children who may not be of their flesh yet are of their hearts. What a picture of God's love for us!

"We love because he first loved us" (1 John 4:19). When the time was ripe, God redeemed us who "were under the law, that we might receive the adoption of sons" (Galatians 4:5 KJV). "Yet to all who did receive him, to those who believed in his name, he gave the right to become children of God" (John 1:12). "For as many as are led by the Spirit of God, they are the sons of God. For ye have not received the spirit of bondage again to fear; but ye have received the Spirit of adoption, whereby we cry, Abba, Father" (Romans 8:14–15 KJV).

Just as Jean chose to adopt Shocka, Oreo, and Fern (and not vice versa), so the Lord has graciously chosen to adopt us. "You did not choose me," Jesus said, "but I chose you" (John 15:16). Now "we wait eagerly for our adoption to sonship, the redemption of our bodies" (Romans 8:23). Someday soon our adoptive process will be complete. We will be home forever with our heavenly Father.

> Someday soon our adoptive process will be complete. We will be home forever with our heavenly Father.

Gordie

Jerusalem remembers. . .when her people fell into enemy hands,
there was no one to help her.

LAMENTATIONS 1:7

Gordie, a stray cat with pale green eyes, was the neighborhood beggar. She had no home that Lynette knew of, but she made friends with everyone she met. Always looking for handouts, she invariably came to Lynette's porch, where she knew she could get a meal no matter what. One night Gordie plodded up the outside steps and simply sat there, unmoving.

"I think Gordie must have been playing in the creek," Lynette's husband said. "She's got a face full of mud."

Lynette went out to take Gordie some food. Mud is not what covered the tabby's face. It was blood. Caked on and dried, the old blood showed Gordie had been severely injured some time earlier. She had come to the one place she knew she could receive help.

Rushed to a veterinarian, Gordie received vigorous fluid resuscitation and eventual surgery to repair her badly fractured jaw. It was a long, costly hospitalization, but Gordie made a full recovery.

Lynette and her husband now have one more cat in their household. And Gordie has a permanent, loving home.

There are few sources of unequivocal, guaranteed help when needed. David said, "Some trust in chariots and some in horses" (Psalm 20:7). Another psalmist declared, "A horse is a vain hope for deliverance; despite all its great strength it cannot save" (33:17). "Woe to those who go down to Egypt for help," Isaiah declared to his people (Isaiah 31:1). Big armies and big alliances do not ensure good help, either.

When we receive a frightening diagnosis, is our first response to pray—or to call a surgeon? When things don't go our way, do we do a spiritual inventory or whine to our friends? In a national crisis, do we simply adopt a "chin up" attitude, or do we humbly seek the face of God? (See 2 Chronicles 7:14.) Job's friends "proved to be of no help" in his time of suffering and loss (Job 6:21). Do we have similar "friends"?

Where can we, like Gordie, truly find help every time?

God says He is our unfailing source of help. In the portions from the two psalms quoted above, contrasts immediately follow. David concluded, "But we trust in the name of the LORD our God" (Psalm 20:7). The writer of Psalm 33 declared, "But the eyes of the LORD are on those who fear him, on those

> God says He is our unfailing source of help.

whose hope is in his unfailing love" (verse 18). Quoting the Psalms, the writer of Hebrews says, "The Lord is my helper" (Hebrews 13:6; Psalm 118:7).

If you find yourself helpless and alone like Gordie once did, remember there is One who is always ready and able to help. You don't need to go door-to-door looking for solace from "gods that are not gods" (Jeremiah 5:7). You don't need to despair without hope. You don't have to climb any steps bloodied and bruised. You only need cry out, "Help me, LORD my God" (Psalm 109:26).

Sam

But when this priest had offered for all time one sacrifice for sins, he sat down at the right hand of God.

HEBREWS 10:12

Sam suffers from convergent strabismus; he's cross-eyed. His beautiful blue eyes hint at some Siamese ancestor, but that's the extent of Sam's telltale Siamese coloring. He is a mixed breed with a striped gray coat. He looks like a cat from an old black-and-white movie—whose eyes have been computer colorized. Through those striking eyes Sam watched Birdie without approaching her.

Birdie was the house sitter for Sam's folks. For three days Birdie did what she had been hired to do. She faithfully watered her employers' expansive flower garden, but Sam did not approach her. He watched from a distance. Was she friend or foe?

On the third day, Sam brought a gift to Birdie as a peace offering. From that moment he waited for her arrival each morning. He rubbed against Birdie in warm welcome and gratefully received a small, daily treat. Like a friendly shadow, Sam followed Birdie around the garden as her attentive companion.

Sam made his peace with Birdie, the stranger who came to his home. But Birdie told him time and again that he need not bring any more peace offerings. One dead rat was offering enough.

God decreed the practice of several different offerings for His people in the Old Testament. Among these offerings are peace, or "fellowship," offerings. After God gave the Ten Commandments at Mount Sinai, He told Moses: "Make an altar of earth for me and sacrifice on it your burnt offerings and fellowship offerings" (Exodus 20:24). As part of their worship, God expected His people to bring offerings that reflected His unique relationship to them and theirs to Him. The peace offering was one of fellowship—a sharing in the blessings of communing with their providing, forgiving God.

Christ came as the fulfillment of the Law and its requirements. Christ not only made peace between God and His chosen people; He bridged the gap between God and humankind—and between people. Christ "came and preached peace to you who were far away [non-Jews] and peace to those who were near [the Jews]" (Ephesians 2:17). "For he himself is our peace," the Bible tells us, "who has made the two groups one. . . . His purpose was to create in himself one new humanity out of the two, thus making peace, and in one body to reconcile both of them to God through the cross" (verses 14–16). Who would have thought that centuries of simple peace offerings were painting such a powerful, all-encompassing picture of a future reality?

Like Sam bringing Birdie his own kind of peace offering, so were God's people in bringing their meager, yet all-important, ordained fellowship offerings. As Birdie then gave back to Sam an offering that was pleasant, practical, and sustaining, how like God, who gave us His Son for our reconciliation to Him!

It's something like those brilliant blue eyes in the old black-and-white movie, something surprising and unexpected.

> Who would have thought that centuries of simple peace offerings were painting such a powerful, all-encompassing picture of a future reality?

Billy.

When they came up out of the water, the Spirit of the Lord
suddenly took Philip away, and the eunuch did not see him
again, but went on his way rejoicing.

Acts 8:39

*B*illy the cat has a damaged larynx. He cannot utter a sound. But Billy is extremely curious. His owner, Paula, has been protective of him for those two reasons. Their neighborhood has a lot of dogs, so she has been vigilant in keeping Billy in the house and out of harm's way. Late one summer afternoon, however, Billy got out. Paula was frantic with worry.

What if he got trapped in someone's garage?

What if someone picked him up?

What if one of the neighbors' dogs got him?

Billy could not mew for help. His curiosity would surely land him in a bad situation. Paula grew more worried, but her search was fruitless. As she stood on her front porch, she cried out her woes to her brother. Then an amazing sight met her eyes.

A golden retriever came bounding across her front yard. The loping dog was wild eyed.

There was Billy, riding on the back of the big dog, having a glorious romp! Paula's frenetic worrying was for naught. Billy was having as much fun as the Lone Ranger sprinting across open country on his horse, Silver. The barking dog may have been distraught, but mute Billy was enjoying the ride of his life!

As Billy's method of transportation was unconventional, so too was Philip the evangelist's after he had shared "the good news about Jesus" and baptized the Ethiopian eunuch (Acts 8:34–40). In a flash, Philip was twenty miles north of where he had been. Sometimes God uses unconventional means to spread the Gospel.

Paul, a Korean Buddhist who lived in the United States and came to know the Lord as his Savior through the ministry of a local church evangelism team, became a zealous Christian. Within a year of his own conversion, he was out evangelizing and leading people to Christ just as he had been led. Suddenly, he lost his job. He was forced to relocate to another state.

Paul immediately began looking for a church where he could continue in lay evangelism. He found a church that had a lay evangelism ministry like his first church. He went to talk with the pastor, who listened to Paul with a look of rapt amazement.

"You are an answer to prayer," he said, his smile stretching across his face.

Paul looked at him questioningly.

The pastor went on excitedly. "We have a Korean congregation that meets here in our building. They have been praying vigilantly for someone to help them reach their own people in their native language here in the United States."

> As the psalmist asked, "Who is like you, God?" (Psalm 71:19). Who, indeed?

A cat riding on the back of a dog. An evangelist miraculously whisked away. A Korean engineer relocated to a state hundreds of miles away—to just the right congregation.

As the psalmist asked, "Who is like you, God?" (Psalm 71:19).

Who, indeed?

Solomon and Sara

*I*t was a good plan, sure to give him some extra spending money. Terry paid a lot of money for two purebred kittens, complete with "papers." Solomon was a beautiful seal point Himalayan cat. Sara was a fluffy gray Persian. Breeding the two cats was Terry's plan. Their offspring would fetch a decent price, and he would easily recover his initial expenditure for his pricey purrers.

Sara finally reached maturity and became pregnant. There was a problem, however. Terry took his ailing Persian to the veterinarian. The news was not good. Sara had developed a very bad infection. In order to save her life, the unborn kittens had to be sacrificed. To make matters worse, Sara had to undergo a hysterectomy. She would never be able to have a litter.

Necessity being the mother of invention, Terry went to plan B. He loaned Solomon to a breeder to sire his pedigreed female cat. Terry planned to eagerly await the news that Solomon was the expectant father of quadruplets, quintuplets, or even sextuplets.

Solomon did not become an expectant father. Shy Solomon, who was born with an incredibly timid disposition, did not breed his new mate. He took one look at her and ran and hid. After the other would-be breeder had to tear open a wall to get Solomon out, he called Terry to come and get his neurotic cat.

Terry's plans came to naught. Neither Solomon nor Sara would ever leave anything behind—except maybe a hair ball or two.

Our plans don't always produce our intended or hoped-for results. "Plans fail for lack of counsel," said King Solomon (Proverbs 15:22). The psalmist observed that when men die, "on that very day their plans come to nothing" (Psalm 146:4). Paul told the Corinthian believers he made plans to return to see them, but prayerful reconsideration dictated otherwise (2 Corinthians 1:15–2:1). Our plans change for any number of different reasons. Often we have no control over the changing of those plans.

God's plans are not like ours. "But the plans of the LORD stand firm forever, the purposes of his heart through all generations" (Psalm 33:11). God Himself reiterates these words in Isaiah: "The LORD Almighty has sworn, 'Surely, as I have planned, so it will be, and as I have purposed, so it will happen'" (Isaiah 14:24). God's plans are never frustrated. From beginning to end God has planned it all.

We are the fortunate recipients of His wonderful plan. As people who live after Jesus walked on the earth, we have the great heritage of godly predecessors like Noah, Moses, and David. "God had planned something better for us so that only together with us would they be made perfect" (Hebrews 11:40).

> From beginning to end God has planned it all.

"LORD, you are my God; I will exalt you and praise your name, for in perfect faithfulness you have done wonderful things, things planned long ago" (Isaiah 25:1).

Sawyer

If anyone loudly blesses their neighbor early in the morning,
it will be taken as a curse.

PROVERBS 27:14

*G*retchen heard a meow so loud it approached a roar. Noises are more easily distinguished when there isn't a busy neighborhood or a bustling street creating a cacophony of sound. Gretchen went to investigate. She expected to find a cat roughly the size of her compact car. That's when she came upon Sawyer.

Sawyer is a little orange cat—Gretchen describes him as "itty-bitty"—who hasn't grown much since that day he first wandered into her yard. She doesn't know if he was dropped off or if he strolled in from another farm, but there he was. He was very loudly making his presence and needs known.

Any cat this small making that much noise is a keeper, she thought.

Gretchen scooped up the kitten with the megaphone meow and took him in as her own.

A born "talker," Sawyer is as personable and friendly as he can be. When Gretchen is home, Sawyer is in constant communion with her. If Gretchen is quietly going about her everyday tasks, Sawyer meows quietly. If Gretchen is excited, his mewing becomes boisterous. If Sawyer is in another room by himself, he's still "talking." Sawyer is never at a loss for meows. Sawyer's kitty chatter is as natural (and constant) as his breathing.

Now that Gretchen has acquired Annie, her new cat, Sawyer is busy teaching Annie the art of communication. Gretchen doesn't know if Annie will ever be able to match Sawyer's Big Volume Voice. But since they are both indoor cats, Gretchen hopes Annie won't.

Have you ever had a neighbor who "blesses [you] early in the morning" with a little more volume than is necessary? Or have you or a friend ever had the experience of talking with someone of another language and finding yourself talking *louder* instead of *slower* to be understood? Ever spent a rainy afternoon babysitting young children only to have to continually remind them, "Children! Let's use our inside voices"?

In the Bible there are numerous accounts of loud speaking. Elijah taunted the false prophets of Baal when their god did not send down fire from heaven. " 'Shout louder!' he said. 'Surely he is a god! Perhaps he is deep in thought, or busy, or traveling. Maybe he is sleeping and must be awakened' " (1 Kings 18:27). After a full day of shouting, dancing, and slashing themselves "until their blood flowed" (verse 28), "there was no response, no one answered, no one paid attention" (verse 29).

Elijah "repaired the altar of the LORD, which had been torn down" (verse 30). After drenching the prepared sacrifice and the altar with water, the Bible says nothing about Elijah shouting or even speaking loudly. It says that "at the time of sacrifice, the prophet Elijah stepped forward and prayed" (verse 36).

> It is only the one true God who says, "Before they call I will answer" (Isaiah 65:24).

Unlike Sawyer, we don't have to call out loudly for God to hear us. It is only the one true God who says, "Before they call I will answer" (Isaiah 65:24).

The Ten

"For he is the living God. . . . He rescues and he saves;
he performs signs and wonders in the heavens and on the earth.
He has rescued Daniel from the power of the lions."
Daniel 6:26–27

Ten mewing, scrawny kittens were about to be eliminated. Michele, an avid rescuer of animals big and small, wild and tame, couldn't bear the thought of the ten kittens being killed. Their owner didn't want to be bothered with putting up a sign reading Free Kittens. She didn't want to listen to their constant mewing. And she certainly didn't want to have to feed and care for them. Michele scooped them up one by one and placed them in a box.

"I'll take them off your hands and find a home for them," she said. She loaded the box in her small car and drove off. She sighed with relief and smiled as she heard the kittens mewing and moving around in their temporary home.

"You'll be home soon, guys," she told them. "It's a big farm with a big barn, and you'll have the time of your lives!"

Suddenly, there was a cat on the seat beside her.

Oops. One got out.

Then another kitten stuck his head out from under the passenger seat.

Another jumped up on the dash. One climbed up on the headrest. Soon, all ten kittens were all over the car, investigating every square inch and oblivious to their rescuer, who was laughing heartily as she drove down the road, surrounded by the curious kitties who were behind her, in front of her, beneath her, and on her.

King Darius was called to account for one of his own decrees. Though "greatly distressed" and "determined to rescue Daniel," the king had to submit to the law (Daniel 6:14). He had Daniel, his trusted adviser, thrown into the lions' den. His final words to Daniel were: "May your God, whom you serve continually, rescue you!" (verse 16).

"And when Daniel was lifted from the den, no wound was found on him, because he had trusted in his God" (verse 23). God did rescue Daniel.

> God is in the business of rescuing.

Stephen, "a man full of faith and of the Holy Spirit," trusted God, too (Acts 6:5). But one chapter later in Acts he was dead, stoned to death for his faith (7:54–60).

God is in the business of rescuing. Peter tells us that "the Lord knows how to rescue the godly from trials" (2 Peter 2:9). Yet rescue is God's prerogative. One of the most powerful statements of faith in the Bible is that of

Job. After losing it all, Job still entrusted himself to God. "Though he slay me," he said of God, "yet will I hope in him" (Job 13:15).

We may have to look ahead for our ultimate rescue when short-term rescues seem to be in short supply. But the God Job trusted in thousands of years ago remains trustworthy today. He has demonstrated it in the sacrifice of Himself. Christ "gave himself for our sins to rescue us from the present evil age" (Galatians 1:4). Our rescuer is close at hand.

Hudson and Wingate

The boys grew up, and Esau became a skillful hunter,
a man of the open country, while Jacob was content
to stay at home among the tents.

GENESIS 25:27

Hudson and Wingate are as unalike as twin cats can be. Hudson has short fur and is a striped golden tabby. Wingate (named for the plumbing inspector who came on the day Wingate showed up at the back door) has long gray fur that has to be trimmed at regular intervals. Both kittens arrived unannounced at Mark's back door. Mark had been in his new country home for one week. Hudson arrived on day eight; Wingate arrived on day ten. They were probably "drops," left in the country by someone who no longer wanted them. However they got there, the kittens needed a home, and Mark needed a mouser. The "girls" had themselves a new home; Mark got two mousers.

Hudson and Wingate soon showed they were more different than alike. Although their primary care veterinarian was sure they were from the same litter, the two cats in no way looked or acted alike. Wingate likes to roam far from home; Hudson stays around the house.

Wingate cares little about people; Hudson is a people lover. Wingate is pure feline; Hudson is almost canine in her habits. If Mark goes for a walk, Hudson walks right alongside him like a loyal dog.

The ultimate difference showed itself as the cats matured. Wingate the wanderer chose to join herself to another family. Hudson the homebody is still Mark's shadow. She's staying right where she is "until the cows come home."

Genesis tells the story of Esau and Jacob, twin brothers who were nothing alike. They were distinctly different from the moment they were born. The Bible tells us they were at odds before birth! (See Genesis 25:22–23.) Esau was his father's favorite; Jacob, his mother's. Like Hudson and Wingate, these twin boys were as different as night and day, and their lives played out completely differently. Jacob was a thinker, a schemer, a planner. Esau was a man of appetites who belittled the important issues of life. (Compare Genesis 25:32–34 with Hebrews 12:16; see also Genesis 30:31–43; 32:13–21.)

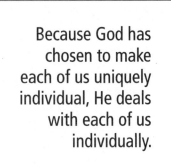

Because God has chosen to make each of us uniquely individual, He deals with each of us individually.

Have you known people like this in your life? Perhaps you and your sister get along beautifully because you are direct opposites. Perhaps you have twin grandsons who never agree on any subject.

Because God has chosen to make each of us uniquely individual, He deals with each of us individually. God says He is the One who gives speech and sight—or doesn't give it (Exodus 4:11). When the Lord healed people, He didn't heal them all the same way. One blind man was instructed to "go [and] wash"; two others were healed with a touch (John 9:7; Matthew 9:29–30). Simon the Pharisee invited Jesus to his house; the Lord invited Himself to the home of Zacchaeus (Luke 7:36–40; Luke 19:5).

Our unique God deals with us uniquely. We need look no further than twin boys, sibling cats, or sister snowflakes. God is "the Maker of all things" (Ecclesiastes 11:5). He is praiseworthy, for each of us—man and beast alike—is "fearfully and wonderfully made" (Psalm 139:14).

Clovis, Patches, and Francis

So God created the great creatures of the sea and
every living thing with which the water teems. . . .
God made the wild animals according to their kinds. . .and
all the creatures that move along the ground according
to their kinds. And God saw that it was good.

GENESIS 1:21, 25

His unusual gray eyes are riveting. Clovis is a long, lean black cat who enjoys sunning himself in the window. There isn't a whole lot that moves Clovis from his private perch—except corn on the cob. Clovis doesn't "do" table food, but he can't resist corn on the cob. As soon as he hears that familiar *crrrunch*, Clovis leaps into the air like he was stuck with a cattle prod. He runs to the table and starts begging like a dog.

Patches is as colorful as a patchwork quilt. His gold, white, and brown splashes of color make him a uniquely distinctive calico cat. Patches loves ice. When Paul sets his empty glass on the floor, Patches makes a beeline for the leftover ice cubes. He sticks his face right down into the glass to get his tongue on that ice. When his face no longer fits, or his tongue no longer reaches, in goes the paw to bring out the ice cubes—one by one—for his personal refreshment.

Julie's cat, Francis, likes to go bowling. Actually, Francis doesn't like to *go* bowling; he likes to *be* bowling. Living in a mobile home with Julie and her family, Francis loves to slide from the kitchen to the back bedroom. He doesn't want to walk or run down the hallway, however. He wants to be "bowled" down the length of it. He comes up to Julie, lies down in front of her, and waits for her to scrunch his four feet together. Keeping him on his side, Julie then gives Francis a mighty shove. Francis skids the entire length of the trailer, looking at everything as he coasts by it. He trots back to Julie repeatedly, just like a toddler on a park slide.

Again! Let's do it again!

"Stop and consider God's wonders" (Job 37:14).

God's diversity in creation is mind boggling. He has made what is seen and what is unseen (see 2 Corinthians 4:18). Elihu said, "How great is God—beyond our understanding!" (Job 36:26). When God addressed Job, He highlighted His creative genius in the animal kingdom. After asking Job some really tough questions, including "Does the rain have a father?" (38:28), the Lord queried him on some observable aspects in creation.

"Do you hunt the prey for the lioness?" (38:39).

"Do you give the horse its strength?" (39:19).

"Does the hawk take flight by your wisdom?" (39:26).

Were He so inclined, God could ask:

"Do you know why one cat likes to be a bowling ball?"

"Why another eats corn on the cob?"

> From the extraordinary to the simple, God shows us His creative diversity in small and mighty ways daily.

From the extraordinary to the simple, God shows us His creative diversity in small and mighty ways daily. "Great are the works of the LORD; they are pondered by all who delight in them" (Psalm 111:2).

Buggy

The soldiers planned to kill the prisoners to prevent any
of them from swimming away and escaping.
But the centurion wanted to spare Paul's life
and kept them from carrying out their plan.
Acts 27:42–43

*B*ecause of her great big eyes, Buggy has a name that fits her appearance. She is an ordinary, domestic striped cat who lives in an ordinary neighborhood replete with an assortment of neighbors, children, dogs, and other cats. As sharp as her big, bug-like eyes are, however, Buggy still fails to see the occasional dog out to do her harm.

Enter Dodie.

Dodie lives across the street from Buggy. Dodie is Buggy's best ally when a dog is on the attack after the big-eyed tiger cat. Everyone is at a loss to explain this unusual truce, but Buggy can—and does—depend on Dodie's protection (particularly from hostile dogs). If ever an angry dog dashes at Buggy, Dodie is there as fast as lightning to protect her. What makes this unusual alliance so peculiar is Dodie herself.

Dodie is not a bigger cat, nor is she a valiant adult

looking after the neighbor's cat. Dodie is not indebted to Buggy for some long-standing favor. Nor is little Dodie a cat-loving, dog-hating child. Buggy's neighborhood ally is a beagle.

She who scares away all dogs from her neighbor, the cat, is a dog herself.

Unlikely alliances are forged in times of trial or stress. Some alliances, like that of Buggy and Dodie, cannot be explained, though the benefit (at least for one party) is clear. As a young girl growing up in the era of the Cold War, I was amazed to watch old black-and-white war movies on television showing Russians and Americans as allies in World War II.

They were our friends? Like other elementary schoolchildren of the 1950s, I feared being bombed by the Soviets when I least suspected it. To ever have, or have had, a loose alliance with the Soviet Union was beyond my comprehension.

As an early Christ follower, Ananias felt the same way. The Lord told him to befriend Saul, whom all knew to be a zealous persecutor of Christians. "Lord," Ananias protested, "I have heard many reports about this man and all the harm he has done to your holy people in Jerusalem" (Acts 9:13). God knew what He was doing. Ananias's alliance with Saul was of His making. "Go!" He commanded (verse 15).

When Paul (who had been Saul before his life-changing encounter with Jesus Christ) was being taken as a prisoner to

Rome, his unlikely protector was the centurion Julius. This noble Gentile allied himself with a Jewish prisoner. It was an unlikely, one-way beneficial alliance—just like Buggy and Dodie's. Yet Julius was committed to Paul's well-being (see Acts 27:1, 3, 43).

> **Be ready for an occasional special, God-ordained alliance to bless you somewhere along the way.**

Some alliances are not spiritually healthy for us and may bring God's judgment (see Isaiah 30:1; 2 Corinthians 6:14). Yet those ordained by God bring surprising benefits. Be ready for an occasional special, God-ordained alliance to bless you somewhere along the way. The Lord doesn't always work in conventional ways.

Blossom

*"God did not endow her [the ostrich] with wisdom
or give her a share of good sense."*
JOB 39:17

*B*lossom loves crunchy cat food. Though he is very young, he has no trouble nibbling away at it until he is quite full and ready to get on with his day. Blossom, though not a domestic animal, is so trusting that he will eat the cat food right from Kay's hand. As much as he likes cat food, however, Blossom is not a cat. He is a skunk.

Blossom showed up one day in Kay's barn and has been merrily stuffing himself on cat food since his arrival. He is as cute as a baby skunk can be with his fluffy tail and black-and-white coloring, and the characteristic waddle of those of his kind. The barn cats have a natural curiosity about him. When Blossom shows up to eat their food, they all begin to gather around, wanting to investigate this new member of their farm family. But Blossom likes to enjoy his breakfast alone. All he has to do to make that clear is change his position. He nonchalantly turns his backside to the curious kitties and raises his fluffy tail.

Zing! The cats scatter like leaves in a tornado! They are

out of there. And they don't look back.

How marvelous the instinctive knowledge the Creator has given to so many creatures! Kay has never had any of her cats exposed to skunk spray, because they know intuitively what's coming if they don't make a run for it. Blossom has never (thankfully) detonated his odoriferous bomb in the confines of Kay's barn. All of Kay's farm animals seem to understand Blossom's method of dealing with possible threats to his well-being, and they maintain a discreet distance.

> **How marvelous the instinctive knowledge the Creator has given to so many creatures!**

In the verse above, the Lord says He did not give the ostrich the same good sense He gave some other animals. Ostriches are neither bright nor nurturing, but they can run like the wind! To the horse God gave strength and beauty (Job 39:19); to the eagle He has given powerful flight and sharp eyes (39:27–29). To the dinosaur God gave "rows of shields tightly sealed together" and a chest as "hard as rock" (41:15, 24). What a Creator of diversity He is!

When your pet learns a new trick, or understands your mood, or mimics what you say or do, remember the Lord who made him that way. It is the same God who provides food for the ravens and endues birds with their migratory instincts (Job 38:41; 39:26). There is none like the Lord God. "In his hand is the life of every creature and the breath of all mankind" (12:10).

Kay did not keep her pet skunk for long. She knew a peaceful, longtime coexistence was a contradiction in terms. She stopped putting the cat food out in the barn, and Blossom took his leave. He hasn't been seen since.

As for the barn cats, they all breathed a collective sigh of relief.

Meazo

*He [Goliath] looked David over and saw that he was
little more than a boy, glowing with health and handsome,
and he despised him.*

1 SAMUEL 17:42

*I*n a dirty, poor, crime-ridden section of the city, Diana found Meazo. The mangy black kitten had been left behind a Dumpster. She was a pitiful sight: barely weaned, thin, and scruffy from one ragged end of her to the other. In spite of her sorry condition and appearance, Meazo found herself lovingly picked up by Diana. Diana took her home, and she and her family nursed the pathetic critter back to health. Meazo had neither the look nor the bearing of a hero when she was found, or even after she was robust with health. But a hero is what she turned out to be.

Everyone had gone to bed for the night. Diana had tucked her boys in, had let Meazo out and back in again, then snuggled in next to her husband for what she thought would be a peaceful night's sleep. Everything was quiet in their mobile home. The clock's gentle ticking lulled Diane into instant slumber.

"Meeeoooow! Meeeoooow!"

Diana rolled over. Was that Meazo? Ignoring the wailed meows, Diana pulled the covers up higher. Her eyelids drifted closed again. . . .

"Meeeoooow!"

Then. . .*whump!*

Meazo was up on the bed, meowing right into Diana's face.

Grumbling, Diana got up out of bed to let Meazo out again, vowing to leave her out the rest of the night. Diana walked into the living room. She doesn't remember if she smelled it or saw it first.

The electrical cord and carpet under the fish tank were smoldering. Smoke was making its deadly way through their home. Flames were about to lick their way up the draperies. Meazo, who had sounded the alarm, stood by quietly as Diana hurriedly put out the fire.

Heroes come in all sizes and shapes. David was but a boy when he heard a giant ridicule the Lord God and the armies of Israel. David alone took up the challenge—not the king who was "a head taller than" any other Israelite (1 Samuel 9:2). Not Abner, King Saul's chief of staff (14:50). Not David's

> **Heroes come in all sizes and shapes.**

oldest brother who served in Saul's army (17:13, 28). It was young David, "little more than a boy" (17:42).

To look at Jesus Christ, God's Son come in the flesh, none would think He fit the heroic profile. Isaiah tells us that Jesus would have "no beauty or majesty to attract us to him, nothing in his appearance that we should desire him" (Isaiah 53:2). Peter, speaking in Jerusalem during the Pentecost that followed the Lord's death and resurrection, said, "God has made this Jesus, whom you crucified, both Lord and Messiah" (Acts 2:36).

Few would think that a bedraggled cat would become a family's deliverer. Not many would guess a boy with a slingshot and five stones would turn the tide of a war (1 Samuel 17). Sadly, countless millions have missed the truth that a baby lying in a manger became the Savior of humankind.

True heroes seldom look the part.

Putting Off the Old Self

*After scolding one's cat one looks
into its face and is seized by the ugly
suspicion that it understood every
word. And has filed it for reference.*

CHARLOTTE GRAY

Snow E White

"The pride of your heart has deceived you."

OBADIAH 3

*I*t's time to hear a tale from one of the cats themselves.

My name is Snow E White. My pets, from whom I acquired my last name, usually call me Snowy. My name fits me well. I have a beautiful white coat as pristine as freshly fallen snow on the dormant rosebushes. Up until *that Christmas* my home was my castle. Then *he* came along.

My pets, Hal and Connie, aren't as discriminating as they should be. They welcome just about anyone in. Including him. Ragamuffin.

Muffy, as they prefer to call him, showed up howling and carrying on at our front door. Such a disgusting racket I have never heard in all my life. I went over to the door and gave Hal what I thought was my most forbidding look.

Don't open this door! Don't!

Of course, he did anyway. And there he sat. That reprobate, Ragamuffin.

The only thing worse than the noises Ragamuffin

was making was his appearance. He was clearly not a dog of breeding, but a mix of this, that, and the other thing. (Whatever "the other thing" was, I couldn't begin to guess.) Hal and Connie brought him in, making over him like he was Lassie or Rin Tin Tin or Scooby-Doo himself.

I flicked my tail in suspicion. Then it was as if Ragamuffin saw me for the first time.

Mom?!

I thought I would expectorate a hair ball right then and there.

Look again, dog breath, I hissed. *I'm no more your mother than that chair over there.*

My look of disgust was lost on Hal and Connie. Ragamuffin was with us to stay.

In the small book of Obadiah is the prophecy against the city of Petra, or Sela, nestled high above the countryside around it. Because of the sin of pride, Sela was destroyed. The people of Edom had looked down on their brothers (Obadiah 12). For their sin God said He would bring them down (verse 4).

"The LORD detests all the proud of heart" (Proverbs 16:5). "Where there is strife, there is pride" (13:10); "Pride goes before destruction" (16:18); "Pride brings a person low" (29:23). If there is anything we must guard against, it is pride. "Do not be proud, but be willing to associate with people of low position" (Romans 12:16). It is the humble whom God elevates (Luke 1:52).

Both Peter and James learned humility in the course of their lives. Both of them quoted the same verse from Proverbs to warn us about pride: "God opposes the proud but shows favor to the humble" (James 4:6; 1 Peter 5:5; Proverbs 3:34). Those are noble words to repeat, but they're not always easy words to live—even as we grow older. Maybe especially as we grow older.

It's time Snowy finished her story. . . .

Ragamuffin and I grew old together. He eventually figured out that I wasn't his mother. I eventually decided he was okay in his place. . .as long as his place was far away from me.

Nicodemus

The apostles gathered around Jesus and reported to him
all they had done and taught.
Then, because so many people were coming and going
that they did not even have a chance to eat,
he said to them, "Come with me by yourselves
to a quiet place and get some rest."

Mark 6:30–31

*N*icodemus is a hardworking cat. He enjoys working in the garden alongside Herb as well as giving Herb's wife, Rose, the benefit of his company when she is hanging laundry. A short Siamese cat with the blue eyes typical of his breed, Nicky is always engrossed in some task.

Nicky keeps busy around Herb and Rose's property. A passionate hunter, Nicky chases down lizards and gophers. He has been known to get into the foxtails in search of his prey. In his zealous hunting he once almost lost an eye to an errant foxtail seed. His veterinarian was able to save the affected eye. Nicky immediately returned to his intensive daily routine. He goes after gophers by sticking one paw as far down the gopher holes as possible. He is relentless in his pursuit of the pests. He sets himself out to single-handedly eradicate them. Nicky moves quickly from task to task. Not one to lounge about, Nicodemus intently hunts, gardens, and socializes.

Nicky once assumed the position of copilot on a long vacation. He climbed up on Herb's shoulder in the car and meowed what was undoubtedly a continual litany of questions.

Where are we going?
Why are we going?
Aren't you going too fast?
I want to go back home!

That long trip in the car was Nicky's last one. He did not protest being left home alone after six hours of constant howling on his one long-distance trip. Yes, Nicodemus is one very busy cat.

Yet once in a while even Nicky takes a break. Rose says Nicky loves to "flirt with the butterflies." He is captivated by the colorful creatures that flutter about the yard's flowers in unhurried flight. It is the one time he drops his myriad tasks to simply sit.

In Mark 6 Jesus sends out His twelve apostles to preach, heal, and free victims from demon possession (verses 7–13). In a parallel account of this event, the Lord forewarns His men that theirs will not be an easy task. "I am sending you out like sheep among wolves," He says (Matthew 10:16).

When the apostles returned from their adventure, it's safe to assume they were exhausted. But there was no time to recuperate. There wasn't even time to eat! Until Jesus intervened for them.

How we need to rest from our busy lives. We are not "programmed" to be constantly on the go. From the very beginning God set aside a day of rest (Genesis 2:2–3). Jesus affirmed its importance when He said, "The Sabbath was made for man, not man for the Sabbath" (Mark 2:27).

> From the very beginning God set aside a day of rest (Genesis 2:2–3).

Feeling like "something the cat dragged in"? Take time to rest today.

Make time to flirt with the butterflies.

Mama Kitty

*I will lie down and sleep, for you alone,
LORD, make me dwell in safety.*

PSALM 4:8

Mama Kitty was a stray cat who called the world her home. Never attaching herself to a human being, she raised litter after litter of kittens under a duplex. Michele watched Mama Kitty and her broods from her own duplex across a small meadow. Using food for persuasion, Michele was finally able to induce Mama Kitty to live under her duplex with her kittens. Mama Kitty remained at arm's length, but on rare occasions Michele was able to pick up the kittens and find homes for them. This cycle repeated itself a number of times until Michele had to move.

Eager to provide for the great golden-eyed mother cat and her current litter, Michele found a ranch family that was willing to provide a good home for some skilled mousers. One thing went awry when Michele released all the cats in the confines of the Ponde Roacha barn. Mama Kitty shot out of her cage like a rocket on the Fourth of July. She ran out of the barn and right into two big, cat-hating dogs.

Mama Kitty had left the safety of the barn and found herself a victim of a vicious attack. By the time Michele and the ranch owner had freed Mama Kitty from the two dogs, the cat was big eyed with fear. Amazingly, her wounds were minimal, but she was covered with dog saliva and was motionless from her ordeal.

Mama Kitty made a full recovery, birthed a few more litters, and was a great mouser. But she ventured out of the safety of the barn with more attentiveness ever after.

We, too, want safety. We move to "safe neighborhoods." We insist on safe schools for our children and safety in the workplace. We long for national safety. Yet safety seems to be in short supply. David prayed, "Keep me safe, my God" (Psalm 16:1). In a later psalm he declared that God would "keep [him] safe in his dwelling" (27:5). Solomon said, "Whoever trusts in the LORD is kept safe" (Proverbs 29:25).

Sometimes we step out of the safety of the barn by our attitudes and actions. In Jeremiah, God's words to His people ring of holy indignation: "Will you steal and murder, commit adultery and perjury, burn incense to Baal and follow other gods you have not known, and then come and stand before me in this house, which bears my Name, and say, 'We are safe'—safe to do all these detestable things?" (7:9–10). There is no guarantee of safety when we live in disobedience to God. Before we plead for safety, we need to make sure our motives and practices are honorable. "The one whose walk is blameless is kept safe" (Proverbs 28:18). "Those who walk in wisdom are kept safe" (verse 26). Just as it was for Mama Kitty, safety is available to us. Nevertheless, it comes within boundaries.

> **Our place of safety rests in obedience.**

Our place of safety rests in obedience.

Oliver

Judas Iscariot. . .objected, "Why wasn't this perfume sold and the money given to the poor?"

JOHN 12:4–5

Oliver is fiercely protective of Jill. This beautiful chocolate Siamese cat with the sky-blue eyes goes into his "guard dog" routine whenever he thinks Jill is in imminent danger. He growls at the supposed culprit and goes to great lengths to defend his mistress. Oliver looks the part of the protector; Oliver also looks like a purebred. But in both cases, handsome, bold Oliver is neither champion pedigree nor champion protector.

In spite of his beautiful Siamese appearance, Oliver is a mixed breed cat. His mother was a purebred Siamese, but she got out one day. As a result of her dalliance, Oliver and his siblings were born. Oliver is the only one of the litter who isn't a tiger-striped tabby.

Oliver isn't all that brave, either. When Jill moved, Oliver went into hiding. It took a while before Jill found him hiding in the fireplace damper. He finally seemed to adjust to his surroundings. Then the new dog came. Oliver disappeared again. Days later Jill found him hiding in the basement. He had climbed inside one of the holy family Christmas statues.

Like an unborn baby, cowardly Oliver was safely huddled inside Mary.

Like Oliver, people are not always what they appear to be. In the Gospel of John, Judas, we're told, was not really concerned about the poor. John tells us Judas had an ulterior motive for objecting to Mary's act of worship. "He did not say this because he cared about the poor but because he was a thief; as keeper of the money bag, he used to help himself to what was put into it" (John 12:6). Although Jesus commended His disciple Nathanael as one "in whom there is no deceit" (1:47), the same could not be said of Judas Iscariot. The extent of Judas Iscariot's duplicity became most obvious when he betrayed the Lord to the Jewish authorities (Matthew 26:47–50).

Paul warns us about "false apostles," men who are not what they appear. "Satan himself masquerades as an angel of light. It is not surprising, then, if his servants also masquerade as servants of righteousness" (2 Corinthians 11:13–15). The Lord Jesus frequently accused sanctimonious religious leaders of being hypocrites (Matthew 23). Among the Greeks of that day, a hypocrite was an actor—a stage player.

Unlike Judas or the false apostles in the early church, we are to be people of transparency, honesty, and integrity. "All you need to say is a simple 'Yes' or 'No,' " James warns us. "Otherwise you will be condemned" (James 5:12). Peter tells us that we are to rid ourselves "of all malice and all deceit, hypocrisy, envy, and slander of every kind" (1 Peter 2:1). Like Paul, we are to conduct ourselves "with integrity and godly sincerity" (2 Corinthians 1:12). This "sincerity" means clearness.

> **We are to be people of transparency.**

Oliver looks to be something he's not. Nathanael was exactly what and who he appeared to be. Choose to be one "in whom there is nothing false."

Frank and Fred

"Certainly evildoers prosper, and even when they put God to the test, they get away with it."

Malachi 3:15

Cherie came home to find her two cats, Frank and Fred, tearing about the house in gleeful delight. The object of their frenzied pursuit was a squirrel. Cherie jumped into the fray with one goal in mind: get the rodent out of the house before it destroyed anything and/or made a monumental mess. Frank and Fred were having the time of their lives. Cherie was half-afraid of the path of destruction that was sure to result if this continued much longer—and half-afraid for her cats and herself.

What if the squirrel was rabid? What if it bit Fred or Frank? What if it bit her?

The mad dash continued with the terrified, trapped squirrel running from room to room. It jumped from one piece of furniture to another. Fred and Frank kept up vigorous pursuit but could not figure out how to trap the varmint between them. Both cats were clearly in pursuit for their own individual gratification.

Finally, Cherie opened the door and left it open. With

a little strategy and a "tightening of the noose," she was finally successful. The squirrel sprinted out the door!

Frank skidded to a stop as Cherie quickly shut the door, barring the fluffy-tailed rodent's return. She looked down at Frank with a relieved, victorious grin. Frank looked back up at her without a victorious grin.

She had let their prey escape!

He hissed at Cherie and walked back to commiserate with Fred about "the one that got away."

Sometimes it looks like the "bad guy got off again." In Malachi's day the people were angry with God. They believed they were serving Him faithfully (though they were not) and had nothing to show for it. "It is futile to serve God," they said. "Now we call the arrogant blessed" (Malachi 3:14–15). It appeared to them that God stood by while the wicked went on their merry way.

Jeremiah wrestled with this same question. "Why does the way of the wicked prosper?" he asked the Lord. "Why do all the faithless live at ease?" (Jeremiah 12:1). The psalmist mourned, "This is what the wicked are like—always free of care, they go on amassing wealth. Surely in vain I have kept my heart pure" (Psalm 73:12–13). Job joins in this complaint: "Why do the wicked live on, growing old and increasing in power?" he asked. "Their homes are safe and free from fear; the rod of God is not on them" (Job 21:7, 9). In the vernacular: It isn't fair!

Often it appears that God just opens the door,

> Someday great and small, righteous and unrighteous, will all stand before God, the One "to whom we must give account" (Hebrews 4:13).

allowing the wicked and unjust to run free. But for all of us a day of reckoning is coming. Someday great and small, righteous and unrighteous, will all stand before God, the One "to whom we must give account" (Hebrews 4:13).

Next time you're tempted to "hiss at God" for the inequities that are all around us, remember that He "will judge the peoples with equity" (Psalm 96:10). And that includes us.

Molly, Max, and Mort

You do not have because you do not ask God. When you ask, you do not receive, because you ask with wrong motives.

JAMES 4:2–3

Molly and Max were two sibling kittens who loved to play together. From the day they were weaned, they never parted. Living on a farm gave them ample room to explore, run, and get into mischief. The only snag in their otherwise idyllic life was Mort.

Mort, the family terrier, had no appreciation or fondness for Molly and Max. He chased them every chance he got, determined to eliminate M and M, no matter what. So great was his obsession that Mort even got hit by a car one day in his crazed pursuit of Molly and Max. The cats kept running. So did Mort. In spite of his accident, he wasn't injured. Nor did he ever stop chasing after Molly and Max whenever he saw either of them. He never succeeded in catching them, but he never gave up, either.

Little Becky, growing up on a farm, never lacked for pets or farm animals. One summer a new kitten showed up in the barn. Becky resolved to catch the evasive critter. She had plenty of cats she could shower with affection, but she wanted this one, too—just one more cat.

She took the stray kitten food and water, but she could not persuade or trick him into coming close enough to pet him. Finally, on a hot summer's day, Becky managed to capture the rascal. Her triumph was short lived. The kitten chomped its fangs into Becky's hand. She dropped the cat quicker than she had scooped him up. He took off running, never to be seen again.

It was weeks before Becky's hand healed, but unlike Mort, Becky learned her lesson. If another cat came along and didn't want to be picked up or petted, it didn't get picked up or petted.

For centuries men and women, like Mort the terrier and Becky the cat-loving farm girl, have had more than enough, yet they've wanted more. The Israelites had been delivered from slavery. They ate "the bread of angels" (Psalm 78:25). They were provided for, yet they complained, "We detest this miserable food!" (Numbers 21:5). As a result, the Bible tells us that God "gave them their request; but sent leanness into their soul" (Psalm 106:15 KJV).

> We must be careful about not only what we desire, but what we ask God for.

We must be careful about not only what we desire, but what we ask God for. As parents are frequently known to say no to their children about the toys they have whined for, begged for, and cried for, so God as our Father often says no to us. It's not because He is lacking in love or generosity, but because He knows best—and quite often we do not.

Don't be like Mort and Becky, heedlessly pursuing cats to their detriment. Rather, learn to "ask. . .according to his will," for "if we know that he hears us—whatever we ask—we know that we have what we asked of him" (1 John 5:14–15).

Bailey

*"Woe to you Pharisees, because you give God a tenth
of your mint, rue and all other kinds of garden herbs,
but you neglect justice and the love of God."*

LUKE 11:42

ulp!

Bailey's eyes grew big. He gasped, choked, and gasped some more. He coughed, he choked, and then he was quiet. All he had done was edge closer to a cellophane ring. His owner, Ellen, had dropped it onto the floor when she opened a container. When Bailey sniffed the ring, static electricity took over. The ring jumped into Bailey's startled mouth. In and down it went.

Bailey began breathing normally again, but Ellen thought she had better take him to the vet. Nothing the doctor did made Bailey worse or better. The plastic culprit never passed. After a series of X-rays, a four-day stay in the pet hospital, and a six-hundred-dollar bill, Bailey was discharged back home in good health. Admittedly, Ellen thought about the inhaled ring every time she made a payment to the vet—and Bailey has remained a bit skittish since it happened—but both of them survived the experience.

Fourteen months later, Bailey coughed up a hair ball with the cellophane ring still intact. He walked away obliviously. Ellen thought of how many other uses she could have found for that six hundred dollars.

I recall the story of a man who had been going to a lot of time and expense trying to figure out what was leaking from his car. He kept checking underneath his automobile, but everything appeared normal. He touched the fluid with his finger and rubbed it between his finger and thumb. It wasn't oily. He smelled it. It had a faintly pungent odor, but he couldn't place it. Finally, he tasted it: just a dab of it on his tongue. His gaze drifted to the corner of the garage. There sat the family cat, looking at him *verrrrry* peculiarly.

He immediately identified the "faintly pungent odor."

Little things in life can cost us a lot in time and resources. Sometimes those "little things" are vitally important; sometimes they are not. Giving such rapt attention to details makes us wish in hindsight that we would have "waited the thing out."

> **Little things in life can cost us a lot in time and resources.**

So, too, with the weightier matters of life. The Lord condemned the Pharisees for attending to the tithing of the miniscule and not giving of their time and resources to people in need (Luke 11:39–42). We, too, can misplace priorities. We go to church, yet we neglect greeting someone who desperately wants a smile or a handshake. We may give money to help meet the needs of people overseas yet not offer hospitality to a foreign student who is alone here in the USA.

Even if you spend money unnecessarily on your cat today—or mistakenly take a taste of something that isn't engine fluid—be ready to give attention to "the more important matters of the law—justice, mercy and faithfulness" (Matthew 23:23).

Buffy and Pumpkin

*A gift opens the way and ushers the giver into
the presence of the great.*

PROVERBS 18:16

Tan and white with long, silken fur, Buffy was rescued
from a trash bin. Back in the days when parents and
teachers were on the same side, a teacher overheard some
boys talking about a kitten they had dropped into a trash
receptacle. Their parents were notified. The boys were
ordered to climb into the trash bin and rescue the kitten.
There was no lawsuit against the teacher, the school, the
garbage collection agency, or the people who put genuine
trash into the bin.

Buffy proved to be a gift-giving cat. He often brought
presents home to his owners. This included an assortment
of mice and baby rabbits. One day, however, he apparently
did some rescuing of his own. The present he brought
home was a small orange kitten. "Pumpkin," Buffy's best
gift ever, was made welcome in the household.

For years after, Buffy and Pumpkin have remained best
buddies. For reasons not known to or understood by Buffy's
owners, he always defers to the younger cat. Whenever

the two of them return home after a full day or night of exploration, Buffy doesn't come in until Pumpkin is safely inside. He makes sure his best gift is not left behind or alone.

Joseph was thrown into a pit by his jealous brothers. They were bent on disposing of him one way or another (Genesis 37:15–24). After pulling him out only to sell him into slavery, the brothers never thought to see Joseph again. But "the LORD was with Joseph" (39:2). After the reunion of disclosure between the forgiving Joseph and his chastened brothers, gift-giving Joseph lavished presents on them (45:21–27).

Joseph's story, like Buffy's, is a snapshot of our gift-giving Savior and God. "God so loved the world that he gave his one and only Son" is the simplest, most profound statement of God's generosity in the Bible (John 3:16). It cannot be said enough—so awesome is its truth, beauty, power, and love.

Sometimes our motivation for gift giving or receiving is not steeped in purity. "A gift given in secret soothes anger, and a bribe concealed in the cloak pacifies great wrath" (Proverbs 21:14). Gifts may only be bribes. They may fool people, but not God. The Lord said, "If you are offering your gift at the altar and there remember that your brother or sister has something against you, leave your gift there in front of the altar. First go and be reconciled to them; then come and offer your gift"

(Matthew 5:23–24). God sees our motivation as easily as He sees our gifts.

Solomon said, "Everyone is the friend of one who gives gifts" (Proverbs 19:6). Not so with the Lord. He told His people, "No longer profane my holy name with your gifts and idols" (Ezekiel 20:39). Our gifts to God are only as good as our heart attitude toward Him. As the Lord has given of Himself to us, we are to offer ourselves to Him (Romans 6:13).

> **God sees our motivation as easily as He sees our gifts.**

Mr. Cat

*"Because you have depended on your own strength
and on your many warriors, the roar of battle
will rise against your people."*

HOSEA 10:13–14

Mr. Cat started out as a bum."

That's how Barbara describes her toothless, over-weight, and "beat-up looking" black-and-gray-striped cat. In his early years Mr. Cat was a rover and a fighter. He had to be put out every night—no matter how bad the weather—or he howled and carried on until Barbara released him. His fierce independence netted him a fight with the dog next door (which Mr. Cat lost) and a stay in the animal hospital to fully recover.

Soon after his hospital stay, Barb noticed a subtle change in Mr. Cat. He had left some of his indepen-dence behind. It came around the time he was diagnosed with diabetes. As a diabetic, he gets two injections daily. Barbara gives him his insulin. She lets him know when his injection is due.

"Mr. Cat, it is time for your shot," is all she says. Mr. Cat lies down and allows Barbara to give him his injections—every day, twice a day, without fail. He capitalizes on his medication schedule by staying around for some extra petting or tummy rubbing.

When little three-year-old Christopher is around during the week, Mr. Cat follows him around the backyard. Christopher's explanation is simple. With a very grown-up air he tells Barbara, "We're getting our exercise." Mr. Cat even allows Christopher to pull him around in his wagon.

The strong-willed, independent, roving pugilist has become happily dependent on his coddling, pampering people.

The prophet Hosea was married to an unfaithful woman. Gomer was determined to walk her own way—out of her husband's loving embrace and into the arms of another. She served as a graphic picture of God's unfaithful people in their relationship to Him. The "land is guilty of unfaithfulness to the LORD," God declared (Hosea 1:2). Like God's unfaithful followers, Gomer said, "I will go. . ." (2:5). Such willfulness brought disgrace, frustration, and punishment. But it also brought out the tender, persistent love of Hosea for his wife and of God for His disobedient people.

"I will show my love to the one I called 'Not my loved one,' " the Lord said (2:23). Because of His great love for us, God seeks those who insist on walking autonomously from Him. "I will heal their waywardness," He says, "and love them freely" (14:4). As Mr. Cat had to come to Barbara for healing and love, so must we come to God. "Who is wise? Let them realize these things. Who is discerning? Let them understand. The ways of the LORD are right; the righteous walk in them" (14:9).

> **For a wayward cat or a wayward person, dependency can be a good thing—a very good thing.**

Independence is not always a good thing—especially if we choose to walk independently of God. Independence has no place when it comes to us and our Maker. For a wayward cat or a wayward person, dependency can be a good thing—a very good thing.

Puff

Puff the pound kitty (Jennifer bought this gray calico from the local humane society) likes to do things her way. When she's hungry, she doesn't meow. She jumps up on the counter and puts her chin on the electric can opener. The whirring noise alerts Jennifer that Puff wants to eat. Puff doesn't always wash her paws with her tongue like most cats, either. She likes to swish them around in the tub whenever anyone in the household is taking a bath.

Every day Jennifer takes her dog for a walk. Puff does not like to be left out of this daily ritual, but neither does she like Jennifer and Brandy's pace. So Puff runs out ahead of them, waits until they catch up to her, and then runs again. This process is repeated throughout the course of the walk.

Perhaps Puff's idiosyncrasies come from being a pound pussycat. Perhaps she was the litter runt. Who's to say? She clearly has an independent spirit. Her approach to life is unlike that of most cats. She has her own unique style and likes to do things her way.

Doing it our way. Marching to the beat of a different drum. Following our own lead. Taking orders from nobody. My way or the highway.

We have dozens of euphemisms to say we want to do things our way, in our time, and at our leisure. From the time we laughingly run away on two toddling legs from our parents, most of us are out to do things our own way. Unfortunately, the problem with doing things our way is that often "our way" invariably leads to trouble.

In answer to his prayer as a young man, Solomon was given unequaled wisdom (1 Kings 3:5–14). "As Solomon grew old," however, "his wives turned his heart after other gods, and his heart was not fully devoted to the Lord his God, as the heart of David his father had been" (11:4). Solomon chose to go his own way when it came to his insatiable appetite for women. In the end, it cost him what was most valuable.

Throughout the book of Ecclesiastes, words of instruction come from the pen of this man who followed his own lead and not God's. Bitterness, regret, and even cynicism underscore much of Solomon's Ecclesiastes. The remaining words of the verse quoted above are heavy with portent. In its entirety the verse reads: "You who are young, be happy while you are young, and let your heart give you joy in the days of your youth. Follow the ways of your heart and whatever your eyes see, *but know that for all these things God will bring you into judgment*" (Ecclesiastes 11:9, emphasis added). There is a price to be paid for doing things our way.

> Delight yourself today in God's leading.

Delight yourself today in God's leading. Follow eagerly after Him who said, "I am the way and the truth and the life" (John 14:6). God's way is the best way.

Misty

You do not have because you do not ask God.

JAMES 4:2

Misty heard the sound that was like the siren's song to her ears. Someone had opened a package of lunch meat. There's nothing Misty likes better than a little snack of deli turkey. But that's all she ever gets—just a sampling. A measly nibble. She decided to change her approach.

Misty did not run to the kitchen when she heard the familiar opening of the refrigerator door and the peeling back of adhesive from the turkey's packaging. This time, she waited. Her owner set her turkey sandwich on the dining room table and went back to the kitchen to get a beverage. Now was Misty's chance!

Misty quickly looked to the right and to the left. Then she silently bounded up on one of the chairs and locked her teeth around a real cat-sized piece of turkey. She pulled the slice of turkey out from between the two pieces of boring bread.

"Misty!"

Too late. Misty took off running with her prize. She was getting more than a measly nibble today!

Hmmmm.

Misty's other passion: Kamryn's Beanie Babies. Misty knows Kamryn doesn't like her playing with her Beanies, but she has sooooo many! Surely she should be allowed to carry around one.

Misty looked up, up, up at the shelving where the Beanies were kept away from her. With practiced stealth, she ascended the shelving. Ever so quietly, she made it to the spot where her favorites were. She gingerly pushed aside the less desirable Beanies. She had her eye on one in particular. . . .

"Misty!"

She had gotten her meal-sized portion of turkey. The Beanie proved a bit more elusive. At least this time.

James warns us about wanting things that God does not want us to have. In the context of the verse above, he says, "You desire but do not have. . . . When you ask, you do not receive, because you ask with wrong motives, that you may spend what you get on your pleasures" (James 4:2–3). If we ask God for that which He wants for us, the results are exactly the opposite. "If we ask anything according to his will, he hears us. . . . We know that we have what we asked of him" (1 John 5:14–15). But there's the rub—His will.

God may no more want us to have a given thing than

Kamryn wants Misty to have her Beanies. There are good reasons for not giving Misty an entire piece of turkey when she wants it, too—even though she may really want it, even though she might be really hungry.

The lesson is clear for us. There are some things God does not want for us. To pursue them is sin. If there's something we want desperately today, it must be in conformity with God's will. If it is, then we can have "confidence. . .in approaching God. . . . And if we know that he hears us—whatever we ask—we know that we have what we asked of him" (1 John 5:14–15).

> There are some things God does not want for us. To pursue them is sin.

Oscar de la Renta

"I was so obsessed with persecuting them that I even hunted them down in foreign cities."

Acts 26:11

$\mathcal{F}$rom the time he was a year old, Oscar de la Renta has had a bizarre obsession. A beautiful cat with the markings of his cousin the tiger, Oscar—because of his peculiar obsession—has had some rooms of the house made off limits to him. These rooms are the bathrooms.

Jordan and her family have learned that Oscar is not a conservation-minded cat. Oscar is quite indifferent to any pleas to conserve our most valuable resource, water. His eccentric fascination gives him cause to dart through the open door of any bathroom in the house at any time of the day. And it's not to take a bubble bath. Oscar is an obsessive toilet flusher.

Whenever and as often as he can, Oscar will sneak into the bathroom, put his front paws on the toilet seat, and then stare for a moment into the watery depths. Then he slowly reaches his paw up to the handle and *flushhhhhhh!*

Putting both paws back on the seat, as the water swirls downward in the bowl, Oscar de la Renta's head swirls in unison. Round and round and round the water goes down. Round and round and round goes Oscar's head. And when it's over?

Up goes the paw. Down goes the handle. *Flushhhhhhh!* goes the toilet.

Round and round and down goes the water.

And round and round and round goes Oscar's furry, striped head.

Keeping the toilet lid down minimizes Oscar's obsessive activity, but only closing the bathroom door prevents it. Maybe there's something to be said for the old-time outhouses, after all.

Paul told King Agrippa that before he became a Christ follower, he obsessively persecuted other Christians (Acts 26:11). There are a number of instances in the Word of God where a person's obsession was to his detriment.

King Saul was obsessed with popularity. When his popularity began to wane, his obsession turned to murderous intent (1 Samuel 18:5–11).

God's name for Solomon was Jedidiah, "loved by the Lord" (see 2 Samuel 12:25). But Solomon "loved many foreign women," and when he "grew old, his wives turned his heart after other gods, and his heart was not fully devoted to the Lord his God" (1 Kings 11:1, 4).

Jesus told a wealthy young man, "Go, sell your possessions and give to the poor, and you will have treasure in heaven. Then come, follow me" (Matthew 19:21). The man turned away. He did not possess wealth; his wealth possessed him.

The psalmist said, "My soul is consumed with longing for your laws at all times" (Psalm 119:20). Of the Lord Jesus Christ it was said, "Zeal for [God's] house will consume me" (John 2:17).

> We can have a holy obsession. His name is Jesus.

Got an obsession? Is it frivolous like Oscar's? Self-serving like Solomon's? Or Spirit-fired like that of Jesus? The Bible admonishes us to be diligent in the things of God, to give ourselves wholly to them, and to persevere in them (1 Timothy 4:15–16). We can have a holy obsession. His name is Jesus.

Snoopie

"But these people have stubborn and rebellious hearts;
they have turned aside and gone away. . . .
Your sins have deprived you of good."

JEREMIAH 5:23, 25

Snoopie is in dire need of an attitude adjustment. When this cat sets his mind to something, there's no changing it—even if it's for his own good. Thirteen-year-old Terra, his owner, learned that the hard way. And so did Snoopie.

This housebound cat decided he would go exploring one day, and out he went without anyone knowing it. After searching all day for her constant cuddling companion, Terra was distraught when ten o'clock came and her daddy told her it was time for bed. The search would have to resume the next day.

Terra was up first thing the next morning and still no Snoopie. She called, she looked, she searched high and low, and still no sign of her beloved cat. Later that afternoon Terra had an idea. Maybe that drainpipe that ran under their driveway near the street. . .

There he was! Relieved down to her toes, Terra called for Snoopie to come out to her. Snoopie would not budge.

The drainpipe emptied into the street. The street had cars going up and down it. Snoopie detests cars. Snoopie is terrified of those deafening, monstrous metal machines. No way he was coming out. No way. Stubbornness met determination. Terra scrunched up her face in thought. She had it! She ran and got a can of Snoopie's favorite cat food.

With the food placed enticingly at the open end of the drain, Snoopie started to come out, cars notwithstanding. Food was in sight! To Terra's chagrin, however, Snoopie was covered with mud and—*ugh!*—spiders. She continued to lure him up to the house with the tantalizing aroma. Finally, she got him to the house, wrapped a towel around his muddy, spider-covered body, and smothered him with joyful affection.

Snoopie's stubbornness was no match for food after his self-induced fast.

The Lord Jesus Christ was angry and "deeply distressed at [the] stubborn hearts" of the religious elite when He was about to heal a man on the Sabbath (Mark 3:5). Later He rebuked His disciples "for their lack of faith and their stubborn refusal to believe those who had seen him after he had risen" (16:14).

There are two different Greek words used for "stubborn" (NIV) and "hardness of heart" (KJV) in these texts. The first is *porosis* and the second is *sklerokardia*. Immediately those in any field of medicine think of our English words *osteoporosis* (hard but porous, brittle bones) and *atherosclerosis* (hardening of the coronary arteries). The callous stubbornness or hard-heartedness of the people in the above scriptural contexts both distressed and angered the Lord Jesus Christ.

> How much better to be like our gracious heavenly Father and follow His instruction.

How much better to be like our gracious heavenly Father and follow His instruction. "And be ye kind one to another, tenderhearted, forgiving one another, even as God for Christ's sake hath forgiven you" (Ephesians 4:32 kjv).

Sarah

"Sovereign LORD, remember me. Please, God, strengthen me just once more, and let me with one blow get revenge on the Philistines for my two eyes."

JUDGES 16:28

Sarah, a fluffy blue Persian who enjoys a pampered life, is not always as docile as she appears lounging about the house. When Kathi, her owner, went to work one night, the couple in the duplex below could hear the *prrrrump, prrrump, prrrump* of four feet tearing back and forth, back and forth, in Kathi's upstairs apartment. The *prrrumps* were occasionally interrupted with a resounding *thump!* as Sarah presumably made death-defying leaps from sofa or chair or table to the floor.

When Kathi married and moved into a two-story house with her husband, Sarah continued her midnight romps. This time she ran up and down the stairs—even when her owners were home. Her wild cavorting was seldom seen. There was one exception.

One evening Sarah got itchy feet to start her after-hours frolic earlier than usual. Kathi watched in amusement as Sarah began running madly about the house, pausing to swish her tail briefly, then taking off at full speed again. Sarah leaped onto the sofa in the living room. She poised herself for a long leap from the sofa to the upholstered rocker across the room. Eyes dilated, hind legs quivering with anticipation, Sarah made a final mental calculation and leaped!

Midway between the two pieces of furniture, Sarah realized she had miscalculated. In a split second the wide-eyed and wild-eyed look disappeared.

Uh-oh.

Whump!

Sarah hit the back of the rocker. She had miscalculated the distance. Her sudden stop was padded, but the romp ended until her headache passed.

Some of us miscalculate all the time. We think we can get from point A to point B and back again before the delivery comes. We sing in the church choir, sign up to help on a committee, and then learn we have two commitments the same day, at the same time. Sometimes we miscalculate in more serious matters. An ailing aunt pleads with us to visit her. We tell her we'll make it Friday. Friday comes and goes; our schedule gets full, and we miss the promised visit. Auntie dies that night. Or we plan to send desperately needed money to some missionary friends. Then there's that big expense on the credit card we forgot about. Miscalculations—our lives abound with them.

Samson miscalculated and underestimated his enemies—morally and politically—throughout his life. When the Philistines finally learned the source of his strength, Samson was overpowered, blinded, and imprisoned (Judges 16:21). But even after a life of miscalculations and poor personal choices, Samson called on his God to make his final calculation the right one, and God honored his prayer (verses 23–31). Amazingly, Samson is even listed among the heroes of faith in Hebrews (Hebrews 11:32).

Done some miscalculating along the way? God stands ready to help us when we, like Samson, repent and turn to Him. He will "revive the heart of the contrite. [He] will not accuse them forever" (Isaiah 57:15–16).

> **Done some miscalculating along the way? God stands ready to help us when we, like Samson, repent and turn to Him.**

Sid

Do not take revenge, my dear friends,
but leave room for God's wrath, for it is written:
"It is mine to avenge; I will repay," says the Lord.
ROMANS 12:19

My human calls me Sid. JoAnn, my somewhat nervous human, thinks I'm the best thing since sliced bread. Unlike some cats, I have a warm home in the winter and cool air-conditioning in the summer. I don't have to hunt for mice or settle for an occasional bug when the hunger pangs start. I just meander over to my food dish and "have at it." Unlike some poor cats, I don't have to share my home with any dogs, either. Allow me to digress a moment.

Any human who thinks cats enjoy living with a dog is a little wet around the whiskers. Dogs are ill mannered, unkempt, and loud. They slurp when they drink, gulp when they swallow, and they never clean themselves up after a meal. If anyone so much as knocks on the door, dogs go into a barking frenzy that's sure to damage the sensitive hearing of any feline. There isn't a cat alive who enjoys living with a dog. They simply endure it.

My only complaint about living with JoAnn is her meticulous care of me. At any sign of trouble, she hoists me off to the vet. After his usual poking and prodding, he usually prescribes some pills for me. I would rather have a shot than have to gag down any kind of a pill. I hate pills. I loathe pills. But pills are what he prescribes. Most recently, however, justice was served.

I had a bladder problem, and so the vet prescribed some pills for me to take. I had already been force-fed a couple of them in the days after my office visit when it happened. JoAnn (did I mention that she is a nervous person?) was in a tizzy about something or other and, in the course of taking her own pills, took one of mine. . . .

I can't say that I didn't relish the look on her face when she realized what she had done. She was none the worse for it. And I had one less pill to choke down.

Ahhhhh. . .sweet vengeance.

It's hard not to gloat when someone who has wronged us suffers. We want vengeance. The contemporary boast for revenge is "I don't get mad; I get even."

The Word of God tells us that God is the avenger (Deuteronomy 32:35; Psalm 94:1). The apostle Paul had an enemy, but he left reprisal to the Lord. He told Timothy, "The Lord will repay him [the man who did Paul a great deal of harm] for what he has done" (2 Timothy 4:14). Paul simply warned Timothy about this man without seeking personal vengeance (verse 15). Personal vendettas have no place in the mind or heart of the child of God.

> Leave to God the business of vengeance—without gloating.

Leave to God the business of vengeance—without gloating.

Beretta

*"I am the only one left,
and now they are trying to kill me too."*

1 KINGS 19:14

*B*eretta was the only "man" in Trudy's life for many years. With his distinctive white face, paws, and tip on his tail, this otherwise all-black cat had the run of the house. Then Ken came along. There was a new man (a real man) around now.

Beretta and Ken got along well for the three years Ken and Trudy dated. The two of them—cat and Ken—were even known to curl up on the sofa together to watch a ball game on television. Beretta was almost as devoted to Ken as he was Trudy. They were buddies. But Ken went home every night. Beretta still had Trudy all to himself most of the time.

Then Ken and Trudy got married. Ken packed his bags and rented out his older home. He moved in with his wife and Beretta. Now when the televised game was over, Ken didn't leave. He was there (when he wasn't working or golfing) all the time.

Beretta took exception to this. His place in the chair

wasn't necessarily his place. His spot in the bed was no longer his spot. Beretta went on a hunger strike, but Ken didn't leave. Beretta continued to pout, but Ken still didn't leave. Beretta came to a realization. His game-watching buddy was here to stay.

Beretta trudged over to his food dish. He sighed heavily before he began eating.

The high life had come to an end when the boyfriend walked out and the husband walked in.

Pouters. They're everywhere!

Elijah the prophet had just triumphed over King Ahab and the prophets of Baal at Mount Carmel. It was an awe-inspiring day of victory for Elijah and the Lord God of Israel (1 Kings 18:16–40). But then Ahab's consort, Queen Jezebel, went after Elijah with intent to finally kill off her nemesis, this "troubler of Israel" (verse 17). Elijah ran for his life. . .and his pity party began. But God ordered him back to work. He told him he was not the "only one left." God still had "seven thousand in Israel" who had "not bowed down to Baal" (see 1 Kings 19:15–18).

When the people of Nineveh repented for their sins and God forgave them, Jonah was not thrilled with the response to his avid preaching. He made himself a shelter, sat down, and pouted because God is a "gracious and compassionate God, slow to anger and abounding in love, a God who relents from sending calamity" (Jonah 4:1–5).

Seen any pouters lately? In school? In the neighborhood? In the workplace? In the house? In the mirror?

Sometimes the best cure for a pity party is a project. Just doing it—whatever it is. We can continue to pout under a bush like Jonah. Or we can go out and find a soul mate, as Elijah did (1 Kings 19:19). Or maybe,

> Sometimes the best cure for a pity party is a project.

just maybe, we simply have to get up and get something to eat.

As it was for Beretta, it's a start.

Putting On the New Self

*When your cat rubs the side of its
face along your leg, it's affectionately
marking you with its scent, identifying
you as its private property, saying,
in effect, "You belong to me."*

SUSAN MCDONOUGH, DVM

Susu

But thanks be to God, who always leads us as captives in Christ's
triumphal procession and uses us to spread the aroma
of the knowledge of him everywhere.

2 CORINTHIANS 2:14

Susu's owner, Lois, acquired a new cat. New Cat, a hulking fifteen pounds, has been cowering under Lois's bed for two weeks. Why? Top Cat Susu, in spite of her much smaller size, has squatter's rights. And Susu knows how to assert herself.

Fluffing out her long, gray-striped fur, Susu looks much bigger and more imposing than her actual size. She methodically struts about the house daily with calculated intent. With the scent glands on either side of her face, Susu rubs her scent on furniture, walls, and objects about the house. She has been so busy spreading her scent around her domain that she has rubbed the fur off the sides of her face. She has balding spots just in front of her ears. The long whiskers above her eyes, the feline version of antennae, have been rubbed down to mere nubs—so intent is Susu on affirming her presence in the house.

Outside of Lois's bedroom, there is not a place New

Cat can go without the aroma of Susu assaulting her senses. Whether she is in the room or not, Susu is everywhere—but New Cat has not made this discovery quite yet.

You see, there's this great big, fearsome, gray-striped cat that sits just outside Lois's bedroom door like a sentinel at the ready. . . .

After 365 days of living in a barge, the first thing Noah did was build "an altar to the LORD and. . .he sacrificed burnt offerings on it. The LORD smelled the pleasing aroma and said in his heart: 'Never again will I curse the ground because of humans' " (Genesis 8:20–21). References to fragrances, aromas, and even stenches permeate the Word of God.

Entire chapters throughout the Old Testament are dedicated to the incense offered in the tabernacle. (See Exodus 30; Leviticus 2; Numbers 7.) Sin and disobedience God calls smoke in His nostrils (Isaiah 65:5). Fragrances and smells are scattered throughout the New Testament as well. Two of the three gifts brought to the Christ child were gifts of fragrance (Matthew 2:11). The fragrance of spikenard lavished on the feet of the Lord Jesus Christ by one woman filled a house (John 12:3). Its aroma continues to permeate time.

> **As Christians we are to be a fragrance in the world.**

As Christians we are to be a fragrance in the world. But, like Susu and her scent, we are not a pleasing aroma to all. "For we are to God the pleasing aroma of Christ among those who are being saved and those who are perishing. To the one we are an aroma that brings death; to the other, an aroma that brings life" (2 Corinthians 2:15–16). Our fragrance should be everywhere we are and permeate all we do. We are to "walk in the way of love, just as Christ loved us and gave himself up for us as a fragrant offering and sacrifice to God" (Ephesians 5:2).

Whoever we "rub up against" today will be touched by our fragrance. Oh, that our fragrance be that of Jesus!

Beauregard

But the fruit of the Spirit is. . .self-control.

GALATIANS 5:22–23

Cats are not the first creatures that come to mind when we think of self-control. Beauregard, however, is not just any cat. He is a cat who must contend with another animal that in any other setting would be his supper and not his thorn in the fur. That animal is Joey, a yakking, aggravating African ring-necked parrot.

Steve has taught Beauregard that he is not even to look at Joey. Water squirted from a bottle has taught Beauregard well. Beauregard does not look at Joey. He knows that even a glance in Joey's direction will get him a soaking, and Beauregard does not like getting wet. Like most cats, he positively loathes it. For Steve (and, admittedly, Joey) this training has worked out very well. Joey can be out of his cage and stroll about the room without a worry about Beauregard making a meal of him.

There is one minor problem, however. Joey is a terrible tease. He can imitate anyone's voice and any number of sounds. For Steve it's the ringing of the telephone. Countless times he's picked up the receiver to hear a dial

always involves sacrifice: sacrifice of time, resources, and emotion. The time and resource elements are obvious, but the emotional pull that we experience as we wait beside another may be the hardest aspect of living out brotherly kindness. In Hebrews we read: "Sometimes you were publicly exposed to insult and persecution; *at other times you stood side by side with those who were so treated*" (Hebrews 10:33, emphasis added). To both groups of believers Christ says, "Persevere"; reward will come (verses 35–39).

Gene and Jo had their son several more months before the Lord took him home. Etched alongside his memory are the dear friends who sustained them with their selfless, brotherly love.

> **From the extraordinary to the simple, God shows us His creative diversity in small and mighty ways daily.**

The cheerful hear

PROV

This cat don't purr."

Janet looked at her new
Janet and her family acquir
they moved to the country. F
Sunny loved the country, an
She was as friendly as she c
in her vocabulary.

Janet tried a number of
Sunny to purr. Catnip, sn
enjoyed them all, but she nev
Sunny must have some physi
incapable of purring. She de
not that Sunny wouldn't purr

One cold, winter day Jan
out in a patch of sunshine o
cat was blissfully soaking up
through the window. Janet lay
her for a few moments.

Ahhhh. Warm sunlight. W
Janet fell asleep, too. When

beside her,
eyes. . .and
Not on!
Hey! I c
"The lo
Janet. The
rest of that
squirrels, e
Sunny

Solomon
but hearta
a minister
you're as j
mind info

> **Nothing**
> **joy or ha**
> **and strai**
> **our coun**

"as scarce
who say t
cats, and
"A ch
dries up

Rascal

"A woman giving birth to a child has pain because her time has come; but when her baby is born she forgets the anguish because of her joy that a child is born into the world."

JOHN 16:21

Rascal had been plodding around the house for days. Heavy with kittens and plump with her pregnancy, she sloughed about in misery. Cheryl, an obstetrical nurse and Rascal's owner, hoped to watch Rascal's delivery.

Before going to bed that night, Cheryl peeked in on her oldest son. Nathan was fast asleep in his bed. But he wasn't alone. Rascal was next to him, very much awake. And there between them on Nathan's bed was Rascal's firstborn.

Cheryl ran and got a mattress and a towel and spread them on the floor. She gently moved Rascal and her first kitten to the "delivery table." Then Cheryl settled in to watch the birthing and lend any needed help.

Over the course of the next few hours, Rascal delivered her additional three kittens. Her delivery was a long process. For the thirty minutes or so between each kitten's arrival, Rascal, according to her kind and to renew her strength,

tone. It's just been Joey "ringing" again. But for Beauregard the torment is not a ringing phone.

"Heeeere, kitty, kitty, kitty!"

Into the room walks Beauregard, eagerly expecting to find Steve or his wife. Instead. . .

"Heeeere, kitty, kitty, kitty! Heeeere, kitty, kitty!" No Steve, no lady of the house. Uh-oh.

Don't look! Don't look!

Beauregard knows it's only Joey. Again.

I can't look! I'll be changed into a puddle of wet fur! It's that Joey!

Beauregard doesn't look. He keeps his head down. He's a study in self-control. But it's hard work.

Self-control is hard work. For some this fruit of the Spirit manifests itself in an uncanny control that many of us find enviable. We are amazed at those unbelievably calm folks who don't go to pieces when their basement floods or the church burns to the ground. We admire moms who don't scream in exasperation when a preoccupied four-year-old

> **Throughout the New Testament we're encouraged to be self-controlled.**

spills milk on the table. We laud the coach who doesn't berate a young athlete who drops the ball he should have easily caught. We applaud for the person who gives up a bad habit—for good.

Throughout the New Testament we're encouraged to be self-controlled. Self-control is needed for prayer (1 Peter 4:7) and for spiritual readiness (1 Thessalonians 5:6). If we desire to be effective and productive in our knowledge of Christ, self-control must be present in our lives "in increasing measure" (2 Peter 1:6–8). To lack self-control is to be "nearsighted and blind" and to suffer spiritual amnesia (verse 9).

Beauregard was fortunate in that Joey was farmed out to a new home. (That telephone trick really got old.) Seldom will the sources that sorely test our self-control be removed. But like the apostle Peter, we may live to see the Spirit bring supernatural self-control to fruition in our lives.

Charlie and E.D.

"Go, gather together all the Jews who are in Susa, and fast for me. Do not eat or drink for three days, night or day. I and my attendants will fast as you do. When this is done, I will go to the king, even though it is against the law."

ESTHER 4:16

How did they do it day after day?

Joe could not understand how it was that Charlie and E.D. (E.D. for the Extra Digit he has on each paw) managed to get into the house from the enclosed porch repeatedly. Even when the cats' private "kitty entrance" was closed, somehow his two feisty felines got into the house proper on a regular basis. Joe determined to find out just how they did it.

With stealth that would make any cat proud, Joe lay in wait one day. The door to the house from the enclosed porch was closed. The kitty entrance was closed. E.D. and Charlie were in the enclosed porch. Joe could see E.D. and Charlie, but they could not see him. Seconds, minutes passed. Then Joe witnessed the remarkable teamwork of his two cats.

Charlie jumped up and held on to a lip that ran

horizontally across the upper edge of the door. Hanging precariously from the narrow edge, he stretched himself out until his back feet touched the door handle. He pushed it down. From his vantage point on the floor, E.D. pushed the door open at the exact moment Charlie pushed down the handle. Charlie released his hold on the ledge.

With precision timing and teamwork, Charlie and E.D. were in the house, the door tightly shut behind them.

Some things can't be done alone. Sometimes we need the help and support of another.

In the book of the Bible that bears her name, Esther had become one of Xerxes' many wives. Xerxes did not know his young bride was a Jew. Esther's guardian, believing discretion to be wise in this marriage over which neither of them had any control, told her she was not to reveal her heritage to the king in whose land they lived as captives (Esther 2:7–10).

> Some things can't be done alone. Sometimes we need the help and support of another.

In the course of time, Xerxes was manipulated into issuing an edict that would result in the slaughter of all Jews in Persia (3:8–15). Esther's guardian, Mordecai, knew the time had come for Esther to reveal her ancestry to the king (chapter 4).

Esther knew that going to the king unbidden could result in her death. Yet she saw no other way for her life and the lives of her people to be spared. Enlisting the prayerful help of others, Esther did what had to be done. The end result was the deliverance of Israel from what would have been a holocaust (5:1–9:17).

We need each other. Paul depended on others for his physical safety (2 Corinthians 1:8–11). Peter depended on the help of Silas (1 Peter 5:12). John the apostle and others were helped by the hospitality of fellow Christians (3 John 7–8).

Teamwork. It gets the job done when one alone is not enough.

Fleck and Family

Welcome him [Epaphroditus] in the Lord with great joy, and honor people like him, because he almost died for the work of Christ. He risked his life to make up for the help you yourselves could not give me.

Philippians 2:29–30

*G*ussie and Paul had been married for forty-three years when they moved to the Kansas plains from Louisiana. In all that time they had never had a cat. But now they were in Kansas country. "You need a cat" was what they were told time and again. A family in their church gave them Samaritan Sam. Sam, as it turned out, would be their first of many cats.

It wasn't long before this couple didn't know how they ever managed to get through life without a cat. Their golden Labrador, JoJo, didn't know, either. He bonded with Samaritan Sam as readily as they did. When a car killed Sam, JoJo grieved right along with Gussie and her husband. All three of them were eager to get another cat.

Several years later Paul, Gussie, JoJo, and their collection of cats moved back to the state of the bayous. When the mother cat suddenly died, Fleck was left as the senior cat. Only a year old himself, Fleck was eagerly sought by the orphaned kittens. This silky black cat with his distinctive white markings on feet and face assumed his role as both father and mother with equanimity. He met the needs of the younger cats. Now when it's nap time, the competition is on for who gets to snuggle in the closest to Fleck. And Fleck is always ready to accommodate his doting brood.

We meet Epaphroditus in the book of Philippians. We know little of this man who was dear to the apostle Paul and to the church in Philippi. Paul called Epaphroditus his "brother, co-worker and fellow soldier" (Philippians 2:25). Although a simple messenger, Epaphroditus also took care of Paul's needs (verse 25). When others were unable or unavailable to help Paul, Epaphroditus stepped in and "risked his life to make up for the help" others could not give (verse 30).

As John and Mary and their two young children returned from four years of missionary service in Argentina, they came only with the clothes in their suitcases. Knowing they would be in the USA for just one year before returning, they anticipated having to purchase a lot of common necessities.

But when they moved into their apartment, Donna and Kathy, two women from their home church, had already been there. All the linens the church had purchased for them had been washed and put in place. The refrigerator was full. The cupboards were stocked. Dishes were ready for use. The medicine cabinet had toiletries and bandages. Their needs had been anticipated and met beyond all their expectations.

Like Epaphroditus with his deliveries, or Fleck with his dual role as mother and father, you may be the one who's needed today. Know that your simplest extended goodness is a "fragrant offering, an acceptable sacrifice, pleasing to God" (Philippians 4:18).

> Know that your simplest extended goodness is a "fragrant offering, an acceptable sacrifice, pleasing to God" (Philippians 4:18).

TG

"Now that I, your Lord and Teacher, have washed your feet, you also should wash one another's feet."

JOHN 13:14

TG stands for Thanksgiving. That was the day Cathy's long-haired calico, TG, came to make her home with Cathy. TG was the runt of the litter and had a rough start in life. But Cathy rescued her from certain death, and TG has been her devoted pet ever since. Smart and playful, TG showers affection on Cathy and attention on Louie, their collie.

Being a dog, Louie does not give attention to some of life's little details like TG does. So TG has taken it upon herself to give Louie some extra TLC. Louie obliges TG by quietly sitting during her feline ministrations. TG grooms Louie. Her scratchy little tongue works methodically, rhythmically over Louie's paws, tail, and even his nose to give him a thorough "bath."

No matter what he undertakes or where he goes, Louie doesn't have to worry about "getting his hands dirty." He has a faithful cleaner-upper to take care of him when he comes home. TG serves Louie in the unique way of her kind.

Before the Lord Jesus Christ partook of His final meal with His disciples, He got up from the table to wash their feet. The customary courtesy of washing the feet of guests was a task given to the lowest slave of the household. When no servant was present to perform the ritual cleansing, Jesus took it upon Himself to teach His closest, beloved followers a lesson in humility and service.

Peter was mortified. No doubt tucking his feet resolutely under him, he declared to the Lord, "You shall never wash my feet" (John 13:8). There was no slave around to wash their feet, and neither Peter nor any of the other disciples had taken the initiative to do what was customary. Blundering as usual, Peter rises to the occasion by—as the old saying goes—putting his foot in it. (In this case, both of his unwashed feet.) Peter refuses the Lord's service. Rebuked with less than a dozen words—"Unless I wash you, you have no part with me" (verse 8)—Peter then goes to the opposite extreme and says, "Then, Lord. . .not just my feet but my hands and my head as well!" (verse 9).

Peter had completely missed the point. His bath—his cleansing from sin—was already complete. The Lord's foot-washing lesson was about service—not cleansing.

"I have set you an example that you should do as I have done for you," Jesus said. "No servant is greater than his master, nor is a messenger greater than the one who sent him" (verses 15–16). Jesus showed His disciples and us that following Him means serving others. "Serve one another humbly in love" (Galatians 5:13). Peter himself later instructs us, "Each of you should use whatever gift you have received to serve others" (1 Peter 4:10).

> **Ready to wash some feet today? Have your towel ready.**

Ready to wash some feet today? Have your towel ready. There's someone who could use the refreshing benefit of whatever gift God has given you.

Morris

For it is by grace you have been saved, through faith—
and this is not from yourselves, it is the gift of God—
not by works, so that no one can boast.

EPHESIANS 2:8–9

M orris, usually a high-spirited, wiry cat, sat motionless before his seven-year-old mistress, Linda. He hung on her every word as she talked to him. As part of her grade school Christian education, Linda was learning how to share the Gospel. She practiced with Morris.

"Morris? You can't get to heaven by being good. The Bible says that we are saved by faith." Linda looked at Morris intently. He returned her gaze.

"Only by grace are we saved through faith. The Bible says we are all sinners. 'For all have sinned,' it says (Romans 3:23). So what you have to do is repent of your sins." Linda's young voice was authoritative. Morris did not move.

"You have to tell God you're sorry, and then you have to show Him you mean it by following Him. You've got to ask Jesus to come into your heart."

Both clearly concentrating, cat and child evangelist

regarded one another.

"Then you do good things to say 'thank You' to Jesus for saving you. Do you want to pray with me, Morris? Do you want to pray and ask Jesus into your heart?"

Linda then prayed with her cat. Again.

Several times a month Linda practiced with Morris, telling him about Jesus and praying with him. Morris listened attentively every time. As Linda's mother concluded, "If ever a cat will be in heaven, it will be Morris."

At the conclusion of Simon Peter's sermon as recorded in Acts 2, the people "were cut to the heart and said. . .'what shall we do?' Peter replied, 'Repent and be baptized, every one of you, in the name of Jesus Christ for the forgiveness of your sins'" (verses 37–38).

> Jesus never turns away any who come to Him in true repentance (John 6:37).

When he was dying on a cross alongside Jesus, a thief had no time left to right his wrongs. His repentance was simple. He admitted he was being justly punished. Then he said to the Lord who hung next to him, " 'Jesus, remember me when you come into your kingdom.' Jesus answered him, 'Truly I tell you, today you will be with me in paradise' " (Luke 23:42–43).

Jesus never turns away any who come to Him in true repentance (John 6:37). The Bible's most famous verse, coming from the mouth of the Lord Jesus Christ Himself, says, "For God so loved the world, that he gave his only begotten Son, that whosoever believeth in him should not perish, but have everlasting life" (John 3:16 kjv).

Have you made a personal commitment to Jesus Christ? As the Word says, "Now is the time of God's favor, now is the day of salvation" (2 Corinthians 6:2). The Lord stands ready to welcome us to Himself. "Here I am!" He says. "I stand at the door and knock. If anyone hears my voice and opens the door, I will come in and eat with that person, and they with me" (Revelation 3:20).

Sierra

Do not forget to show hospitality to strangers,
for by so doing some people have shown hospitality
to angels without knowing it.

HEBREWS 13:2

A long, lush, white-and-burnt-orange fur coat covers this California cat. Sierra makes her home with two single women, Stephanie and Kara. Kara, the Johnny-come-lately in the mix, is the new roommate. Steph has her private quarters and Kara, hers. They share some common space, of course, which includes the kitchen and living room. Sierra, convinced she is the matriarch of the household, is of the opinion that the entire apartment is her domain. So she goes uninvited when and where she pleases—including into cat-allergic Kara's sleeping quarters.

Sierra has gotten accustomed to Kara's presence over the last several months. She no longer sneaks up behind Kara to bite her on the leg. (This was Sierra's subtle method of reminding Kara she was a presence to be reckoned with.) Sierra and Kara have become conversational buddies, though contact continues to be kept at a minimum.

Recently Kara had her midwestern parents come for

a visit. This was not to Sierra's liking. She doesn't like guests who overstay their welcome. For Sierra that means about two hours. By the end of the first day, standoffish Sierra was suspiciously following the visitors about the apartment, watching their every move. On the third day Sierra bit Kara's mother on the leg.

Just a subtle reminder is all. . . .

Sierra does not like entertaining. For her, hospitality is just another way to spell "hair ball."

Abraham recognized unannounced guests of importance when he saw them. He did not need the New Testament admonition above; he lived it! He wasted no time preparing a meal for his heavenly visitors. In the Genesis account of this visit, he hurries to meet them, runs to prepare a meal for them, and instructs his wife to be quick about baking some bread for them (18:1–8).

> Even if hospitality is not what we do best, all the scriptures above make it clear that we are to be hospitable to others.

Throughout the New Testament we are urged to be hospitable people. Paul says, "Practice hospitality" (Romans 12:13). Peter, who hosted the Lord Jesus Himself and numerous other people at one time (Luke 4:38–40), tells us, "Offer hospitality to one another without grumbling" (1 Peter 4:9). The apostle John admonishes us to "show hospitality" to believers in ministry whom we do not know "so that we may work together for the truth" (3 John 8).

Even if hospitality is not what we do best, all the scriptures above make it clear that we are to be hospitable to others. We don't have to go out and get a calf for immediate slaughter or bake a fresh loaf of bread. Even "a cup of cold water" given in the name of Jesus is not without its reward (Matthew 10:42). It is all a beautiful picture of the future when the Master who showed Himself servant of all will "dress himself to serve, will have them [His servants] recline at the table and will come and *wait on them*" (Luke 12:37, emphasis added).

Hospitality?

In the vernacular: We ain't seen nothin' yet!

Roger

"I will send down showers in season;
there will be showers of blessing."

EZEKIEL 34:26

*B*rad looked outside. It was ugly. His tenth birthday party was to start soon, but the storm was horrendous. Would anyone come? Finally, one boy came, then another. Brad was encouraged. When the time came, in spite of the inclement weather, Brad's birthday party was in full swing. The cold November day with its torrential rains in no way disrupted his party. The horrific storm did not keep even one of his buddies away. Oblivious to the thunder, lightning, wind, and rain outside, they were caught up in games, prizes, presents, and eating cake. In the middle of the merriment, there was a momentary lull. Everyone heard the pitiful cry. Jumping up, Brad raced to the front door.

There he sat, no bigger than one of Brad's tennis shoes and wetter than a washcloth hanging in the shower. Although Brad received many gifts, he decided this one was his favorite. He brought him in and kept him as his special birthday gift. The boys named the gray kitten Roger.

Mary, Brad's mother, says they never say it's "raining cats and dogs" anymore. Ever since Brad's tenth birthday, when the rains pour down, it's "raining kittens and puppies."

Doug and Doris enjoy "adopting" international university students while they study in the USA. Not long ago their adopted students, a married Chinese couple, were expecting their first baby. The American couple planned a baby shower for the new arrival. Frank, the baby's father, thought they planned to bathe their infant as part of some weird American cultural practice. When Doris explained they were going to "shower" their infant with gifts, Frank was eager to come to the shower with his wife and baby. To their delight and amazement, gifts were rained on them in abundance.

God promises His people a time when He will rain "showers of blessing" upon them. Although this time is yet future, He showers us now with countless blessings if we take time to look past the thunderclouds and storms of life. On some occasions God sends blessings in the form of deliverance from enemies (Psalm 3:8). Blessings

> **Blessings come when we "live together in unity."**

come when we "live together in unity" with our brothers (133:1–3). The blessing of tithing is to receive ample supply from God in turn (Malachi 3:10).

With God's abundant showers of blessing, we are expected to be productive people of God. "Land that drinks in the rain often falling on it and that produces a crop useful to those for whom it is farmed receives the blessing of God. But land that produces thorns and thistles is worthless and is in danger of being cursed" (Hebrews 6:7–8). Accountability often follows on the heels of blessing. Brad had a cat to care for; Frank and his wife had a lot of gifts to load up and carry home. "Freely you have received," the Lord told His disciples as He sent them out in ministry, "freely give" (Matthew 10:8).

Feeling blessed today? Be a blessing to another.

Igloo

*Remember those in prison as if you were together
with them in prison, and those who are mistreated
as if you yourselves were suffering.*

HEBREWS 13:3

Igloo was an abandoned kitten that Mary Jo had to carry in a cooler to work. (Hence Igloo's name.) No one was home during the day, and the kitten was not yet weaned, so Mary Jo nursed her with a bottle until Igloo was old enough to feed herself.

Never having had a mother cat she can remember, Igloo thinks of herself as Mary Jo's daughter. When Mary Jo got another kitten, Igloo wasn't sure just how to take this strange new animal in their house. To share her thoughts with another, Igloo began "writing" to a man in prison.

Though she has little to say, Igloo's brief notes to her incarcerated pen pal surely brighten his days. Igloo sends him holiday and birthday cards. She describes her friend Woodi the cat (and his escapades) in detail. Igloo doesn't want or expect replies from the man she writes. Communication is one way.

Few people know of Igloo's letters to the man neither

she nor Mary Jo has ever met. No one else need know. The unknown stranger who sits alone in his cell knows.

People like Tom, a Christian layman involved in prison ministry, don't make the news headlines. They go about their service without fanfare, never receiving (or expecting) accolades for the work they do. Yet Christ put a high premium on those who minister to prisoners. He equated ministry to those in prison with ministry to the sick, the hungry, the thirsty, and the poor. Ultimately, it is all service to Him (Matthew 25:34–36).

Both the righteous and the unrighteous will stand before Christ our Judge one day. Individuals in both groups will say to Him: "When did we see you hungry or thirsty or a stranger or needing clothes or sick or in prison, and did not help you?" (verse 44). To both groups Christ will answer, "Truly I tell you, whatever you did [or did not do] for one of the least of these brothers and sisters of mine, you did [or did not do] for me" (verse 40). Jesus Christ identifies with suffering people—even when (it would appear) their suffering is a consequence of their own actions. Our response, or lack thereof, to those who suffer demonstrates the reality of our relationship to Jesus Christ.

> To feed the hungry, clothe the naked, or visit the prisoners is to conduct ourselves like our gracious Maker.

To feed the hungry, clothe the naked, or visit the prisoners is to conduct ourselves like our gracious Maker. "He upholds the cause of the oppressed and gives food to the hungry. The LORD sets prisoners free, the LORD gives sight to the blind, the LORD lifts up those who are bowed down" (Psalm 146:7–8).

We may not be able to do it all, but we can do something. A visit to someone in the hospital, an e-mail to a missionary overseas, a check to a soup kitchen, a letter from your cat to a prisoner—all little (and big) things that are not missed by our big God of little details.

Another Sam

God's gifts and his call are irrevocable.

ROMANS 11:29

W hat have you got, Sam?"

Their repeated routine never gets old. Sam, a beautiful cat with glistening green eyes and gray-and-white fur, is a good mouser. Dorothy only feeds Sam the best of food: tuna and mackerel—never cat food. She's a firm believer in the adage "A well-fed cat is a better mouser." So Sam is fed well. Not only will Sam not eat cat food, but he won't eat the mice he catches, either. Once he kills a mouse, he brings his deceased prey into the house. He waits for Dorothy to pull out her kitchen chair, sit down, and ask *the question.*

"What have you got, Sam?"

Sam drops the dead rodent at her feet, gets a treat and verbal praise, and then goes to take his nap. He would no more think of eating a mouse than Dorothy would. She discreetly picks it up in paper towels. She throws Sam's gift into the garbage.

Yet one day Sam brought Dorothy a gift she could not throw into the garbage.

Dorothy was going about her household tasks. Her daughter, just out of high school and now working, had made a dash out the door that morning. She had not completely closed her lingerie drawer. Dorothy went in to close it, and there was Sam, in the drawer with his latest gift.

Sam was curled up with four new nursing kittens.

God's "indescribable gift" to us is the Lord Jesus Christ (2 Corinthians 9:15). Nothing compares to the inexpressible gift of Himself to redeem us. God's "gift of righteousness" (Romans 5:17) is something we could never acquire on our own; it is only available through Jesus Christ. Yet once we receive that one unequaled gift, God gives even more gifts to us.

We're told that "each of [us] has [our] own gift from God" (1 Corinthians 7:7). That may mean

> Nothing compares to the inexpressible gift of Himself to redeem us.

marriage; it may mean celibacy (verses 1–7). There are gifts of the Spirit as well. These are "distributed according to his [God's] will" (Hebrews 2:4). Whatever gift we have been awarded, we are to share or exercise in the building up of Christ's body, the church. "Each of you should use whatever gift you have received to serve others, as faithful stewards of God's grace in its various forms" (1 Peter 4:10).

No one would fault Dorothy for wasting Sam's gifts

of dead mice, but Samantha's gift of a litter of kittens is something entirely different. Like God's gifts, such a gift should not be squandered.

If you have never received God's greatest gift, Jesus Christ, do so today. "For it is by grace you [are] saved, through faith—and this is not from yourselves, it is the gift of God—not by works, so that no one can boast" (Ephesians 2:8–9).

If you have already received that precious gift, be looking for ways to share your other gifts with and for the benefit of others. You may not get a name change like Sam, but it may be a discovered delight for someone else.

Coyote

You need to persevere so that when you have done
the will of God, you will receive what he has promised.

HEBREWS 10:36

Coyote is not a coyote. He is a common domestic cat with coyote coloring. Being an outdoor cat, Coyote must live by his wits, his God-given abilities to prowl, stalk, and persevere in the hunt. Coyote has a place of shelter in the barn during inclement weather, and he is given just enough processed cat food to keep him strong for the hunt.

Mousing is hard work. It takes perseverance. Coyote scans the yard with his sharp golden eyes. Back and forth, back and forth, slowly he takes in the width of the yard, looking for any slight movement of creature or grass. He may look to be distracted by his morning grooming, methodically licking his paws and rubbing them over his face. Yet he only appears to be distracted. His concentration is elsewhere. . . .

Suddenly, he stops. He sits up taller. He zeroes in on a point more than twenty feet from where he sits. A mouse scurries about the ground, barely visible under a pine tree. Ever so slowly, Coyote lowers his entire body. He sits for a few seconds longer, scarcely breathing, not moving a whisker. Then in his "low slide" position, he begins to close the distance between the mouse and himself.

Two steps. . .stop.

Raise one paw to move. . .and stop.

His right front paw is suspended in midair. He puts it down with practiced slowness.

He waits. He takes three more low, sliding steps toward his prey. . . .

Then, nothing.

His mouse is gone.

Supper scurries down a hole.

Coyote abruptly sits up. He marches over to investigate. She's gone, all right. He knows there's no way he'll fit down that hole. Not looking back, he turns his attention to the adjacent field. He fairly bounces over to the field to watch for another mouse.

> Do you persevere when time, circumstances, or limitations hold your goal at bay?

It's all in a day's work for Coyote. He's ready to persevere in the hunt. Sometimes he doesn't get the mouse on his first try, his second, or even his third. But he stays on task. He perseveres.

Oh, to copy Coyote's perseverance! Do you persevere when time, circumstances, or limitations hold your goal at bay? In the Bible the word translated *persevere* has within its meaning patient waiting. It carries with it the idea of "cheerful (or hopeful) endurance, constancy." That's tough, isn't it? We can persevere; we can endure. But cheerfully? Hopefully? That's a mouse the size of a house! In James we're told to "let perseverance finish its work so that [we] may be mature and complete" (1:4).

When it comes time to persevere (perhaps today), picture Coyote. Not crying about the "one that got away," but bouncing merrily, determinedly off to await his next opportunity. For Coyote it may mean a midmorning snack.

For us it means "endurance inspired by hope in our Lord Jesus Christ" (1 Thessalonians 1:3) and a maturity that brings its own lasting reward.

Abner and Markov

*Now about your love for one another we do not need
to write to you, for you yourselves have been
taught by God to love each other.*

1 Thessalonians 4:9

*A*bner, an all-American cat, and Markov, a feline imported from Russia, had no language hurdles in their private brotherhood. Steve and his wife came back from their stay in Russia with their adopted cat in tow. Abner and Markov played together, slept together, and went out and returned together every night. One night, however, the twosome did not come home. Steve's wife called them repeatedly, but to no avail. She was about to give up when she finally saw them. But something was very wrong. Abner was barely moving; Markov was coaxing him—gently pushing him—toward home.

Abner had been brutally assaulted with a baseball bat. One eye was smashed, and the left side of his jaw was fractured. Markov was uninjured but had prodded his friend home, staying with him until they arrived. Bloodied and swollen, Abner was in shock. Steve and his wife had no time to be amazed by Markov's labor of love.

Steve rushed his battered cat to an emergency veterinary service.

The news was bad. "We'll do what we can," he was told, "but expect to pick up a body in the morning."

Amazingly, Abner made a full recovery. Markov had stuck by him with unheralded brotherly love—and brought him home.

Five people surrounded Gene, Jo, and their grown son in the airport. The son, born with cystic fibrosis, was about to receive a double lung transplant. After the eight of them prayed together, Gene, Jo, and their son boarded the aircraft for their 250-mile trip.

Unknown to Gene and Jo, one of the couples went home and packed their bags. They picked up Gene and Jo's car and then drove that same 250-mile trip in two cars. They came to stay with their friends.

"We didn't want you to go through this alone," was their simple explanation.

Through the long ordeal of transplant surgery and the subsequent postoperative days, Gene and Jo did not have to "go it alone." Brotherly love was lavished on them in an unsought, unannounced, unpretentious sacrifice of mere presence.

Of all the character qualities we are to "add to [our] faith" (2 Peter 1:5), the last one before the greatest of all (love) is "mutual affection" (verse 7). To be there for another always involves sacrifice: sacrifice of time, resources, and emotion. The time and resource elements are obvious, but the emotional pull that we experience as we wait beside another may be the hardest aspect of living out brotherly kindness. In Hebrews we read: "Sometimes you were publicly exposed to insult and persecution;

> From the extraordinary to the simple, God shows us His creative diversity in small and mighty ways daily.

at other times you stood side by side with those who were so treated" (Hebrews 10:33, emphasis added). To both groups of believers Christ says, "Persevere"; reward will come (verses 35–39).

Gene and Jo had their son several more months before the Lord took him home. Etched alongside his memory are the dear friends who sustained them with their selfless, brotherly love.

Sunny

The cheerful heart has a continual feast.

PROVERBS 15:15

This cat don't purr."

Janet looked at her newly adopted, eight-year-old cat. Janet and her family acquired Sunny from a friend when they moved to the country. Her friend's words proved true. Sunny loved the country, and she was an excellent hunter. She was as friendly as she could be. But purring was not in her vocabulary.

Janet tried a number of things for a while to induce Sunny to purr. Catnip, snuggles, toys, treats—Sunny enjoyed them all, but she never purred. Janet decided that Sunny must have some physical defect that rendered her incapable of purring. She decided that the problem was not that Sunny wouldn't purr but that she couldn't.

One cold, winter day Janet noticed Sunny sprawled out in a patch of sunshine on the bedroom carpet. Her cat was blissfully soaking up the warmth that poured in through the window. Janet lay down beside Sunny to pet her for a few moments.

Ahhhh. Warm sunlight. Warm carpet. Warm cat.

Janet fell asleep, too. When she awoke, Sunny was still

beside her, contentedly gazing at her with big, rounded eyes. . .and Sunny began to purr.

Not only was Janet surprised, but so was Sunny.

Hey! I can *do this!*

"The look on Sunny's face was wonderful," recalls Janet. The memory still elicits a smile from her. For the rest of that day, everything made Sunny purr: the sofa, the squirrels, even the furnace!

Sunny has been purring ever since.

Solomon said, "A happy heart makes the face cheerful, but heartache crushes the spirit" (Proverbs 15:13). Don, a minister of music, has been known to ask his choir, "If you're as joyful as you claim to be in this song, would you mind informing your face?" Nothing communicates joy or happiness as simply and straightforwardly as our countenance.

> Nothing communicates joy or happiness as simply and straightforwardly as our countenance.

As purring is to a cat, so is a smile to the human countenance. Sometimes we meet folks whose smiles are "as scarce as hen's teeth." (Smiling grandmas are people who say things like that. Many of them have had hens and cats, and they would know.)

"A cheerful heart is good medicine, but a crushed spirit dries up the bones" (Proverbs 17:22). Peter quoted King

David, saying, "Thou hast made known to me the ways of life; thou shalt make me full of joy with thy countenance" (Acts 2:28 KJV). What a transforming, disarming weapon is the smile! Smiling is universal. It is one of life's most powerful communicators.

Other than discovering that there wasn't anything physically wrong with Sunny's "purrer," Janet learned two other lessons from Sunny that winter day. Purring (or smiling) may result from something as simple as sharing a patch of sunlight with another. No one has to look long or far to find something to smile about—and to give that smile to someone else. And Janet's final lesson from her once im*purr*fect cat?

"Purring is easy once you get the hang of it."

Doing Battle: Everyday Enemies. . . Subtle Snares

*No matter how much cats fight,
there always seems to be
plenty of kittens.*

ABRAHAM LINCOLN

Athena

*I looked up and there before me was a man dressed in linen,
with a belt of fine gold from Uphaz around his waist. His body
was like topaz, his face like lightning, his eyes like flaming
torches, his arms and legs like the gleam of burnished bronze,
and his voice like the sound of a multitude.*

DANIEL 10:5–6

This Athena is not the mythological Greek goddess; she's
an orange tabby who gets herself in—and miraculously
out of—some deadly traps. Athena has no pedigree and
nothing to commend her as a valiant fighter, but she has
shown her young master, Rob, that she can take care of
herself in kitty war zones.

Athena was once caught in a raccoon trap and escaped.
There was no mark on her to say that she had been a
captive. Yet her collar was found in the trap by a neighbor.
How she got in or out remains a mystery. In a world that
is frequently unfriendly to her kind, Athena managed to
best the trap.

Then there was the night Athena had once again
outwitted forces against her. She came home looking
like the creature from the black lagoon. And smelling
like it, too. Covered from head to paws with mud and/or

sewage, Athena's acquired odor filled the house. In spite of an immediate, vigorous shampooing, she continued to reek for two more days. Her drenching in some unknown pit remains a mystery. Yet somehow she had once again escaped. Athena is a soldier of uncommon ingenuity.

Athena is a survivor.

We, too, face battles and hazards in the spiritual realm that are unseen by others. "For though we live in the world, we do not wage war as the world does. The weapons we fight with are not the weapons of the world. On the contrary, they have divine power to demolish strongholds" (2 Corinthians 10:3–4). Those are hard words speaking hard facts.

The prophet Daniel had an encounter with an unnamed angel who had to fight his way to Daniel (Daniel 10:13). For three weeks Daniel had been suffering because of an unexplained vision. For three weeks this olive-green-and-copper-colored being with a "face like lightning" (verse 6) struggled to get to Daniel to strengthen him (verses 2, 12–13, 18–19).

For us, thousands of years after Daniel, the warfare has continued. We may not see it, but we are affected by it. We are in the midst of a battle. To be clothed with the Lord Jesus means we must "put on the armor of light" (Romans 13:12–14). There is not one piece of armor we can be without if we are to best the enemy (Ephesians 6:10–18).

Like sewage-soaked Athena, we may look like we've been through a war. Or—like Athena after her escape from the raccoon trap, or like the unnamed angel of Daniel 10—we may look robust and untainted. Either way, when all is said and done, we will emerge victorious. For "the Lion of the tribe of Judah, the Root of David, has triumphed" (Revelation 5:5).

> For "the Lion of the tribe of Judah, the Root of David, has triumphed" (Revelation 5:5).

Mew

*Hear me, my God, as I voice my complaint;
protect my life from the threat of the enemy.*

PSALM 64:1

Poor Mew had a tough time of it every day. The neighbor cat, Old Vicary, was a bully. Whenever Mew went out, he looked around cautiously. If Old Vicary found him, he boxed him handily every time. Mew was just not the fighter his nemesis was. He always got hurt; he never won in their frequent feline fisticuffs. Going out became a fearful venture—until Mew found the perfect hiding place.

The spot where Mew found safety from his enemy was dank and dark. The ledge on which he hid was precarious at best and dangerous at its worst. But that's where Mew found refuge. He would huddle down until the danger passed. When his owner called him home, he always poked his head out very slowly to make sure Old Vicary was not in sight. He did not want to divulge his haven of safety. Only if his enemy was not around did Mew make a mad dash for the safety of his house.

Where did Mew go?

What was his "haven of safety"?

Mew's place of protection was the last place anyone—especially a cat—would look: in a storm sewer.

The world never seems to lack for bullies. When Nehemiah was overseeing the rebuilding of the walls of Jerusalem, the bullies were Sanballat and Tobiah. With threats, jeers, plots, and intimidation, these two men and their forces tried to stop the reconstruction process (Nehemiah 4:1–9). Queen Jezebel bullied the prophets of God to the point of mass execution (1 Kings 18:4). Paul the apostle was bullied into silence by Demetrius, a silversmith who saw a loss in business profits with the preaching of the Gospel of Jesus Christ (Acts 19:23–41).

There is no ready formula for resisting or fighting a bully. Nehemiah had to use all his diplomatic and military skills to accomplish his task (Nehemiah 1–6). When it was finished, he said the "work had been done with the help of our God" (6:16).

God may give us victory over our bullies, but He may not. Queen Jezebel met her end in a grisly death (2 Kings 9:30–37), but she had already murdered many good men. Paul was forced to leave Ephesus; others had to carry on the work he started (Acts 20:1, 28–31). Neither Paul nor the prophets of God whom Jezebel slaughtered fared as well as Nehemiah.

> God may give us victory over our bullies, but He may not.

We don't always come out the winner. Sometimes the bully wins—like Old Vicary or Demetrius. Our only recourse may be to hide in the storm sewer. When times of defeat come, we still have our loving Father. "He knows how we are formed, he remembers that we are dust" (Psalm 103:14). "But from everlasting to everlasting the LORD's love is with those who fear him" (verse 17).

We may find ourselves holed up in a smelly storm sewer—but we will never be there alone.

Rascal

Rascal had been plodding around the house for days. Heavy with kittens and plump with her pregnancy, she sloughed about in misery. Cheryl, an obstetrical nurse and Rascal's owner, hoped to watch Rascal's delivery.

Before going to bed that night, Cheryl peeked in on her oldest son. Nathan was fast asleep in his bed. But he wasn't alone. Rascal was next to him, very much awake. And there between them on Nathan's bed was Rascal's firstborn.

Cheryl ran and got a mattress and a towel and spread them on the floor. She gently moved Rascal and her first kitten to the "delivery table." Then Cheryl settled in to watch the birthing and lend any needed help.

Over the course of the next few hours, Rascal delivered her additional three kittens. Her delivery was a long process. For the thirty minutes or so between each kitten's arrival, Rascal, according to her kind and to renew her strength, ingested each placenta. She then licked and licked and licked each new kitten with loving intensity, contentedly purring the entire time. When the time came to deliver the next kitten, the purring and licking stopped. Rascal began howling and whining. Birthing is hard work. Once the next kitten was born, the process repeated itself again. Rascal's panting and groaning stopped; the grooming and purring began. Finally, all four kittens were hungrily renewing their own strength.

The birthing had been hard work for them, too.

> Through Jesus' shed blood and the marvelous working of His Holy Spirit, God continues to birth individuals into His family.

For the delivering mother, the one being born, or the one standing by ready to help, new birth means pain and labor (in both senses of the word). In both the physical and spiritual realms, birthing is difficult. Jesus told His apostles that the birthing of the church was going to be hard won and painful. He was about to be crucified. But the time of rejoicing would come (John 16:22).

Christ birthed the church to life in His death. Through Jesus' shed blood and the marvelous working of His Holy Spirit, God continues to birth individuals into His family. The Lord Jesus told Nicodemus, "No one can enter the kingdom of God unless they are born of water and the Spirit. . . . The Spirit gives birth to spirit" (John 3:5–6). Christ suffered like no one before or since to make possible our spiritual birth (see Isaiah 53:3; Matthew 26:36–67; 27:26–50).

Similarly, the spiritual birthing process is often difficult for the newly born child of God. Things like pride do not easily loose their grip on us. And as "newborn babies" (1 Peter 2:2), new believers are up against hostile forces (John 15:18–19). We can't make it on our own. Other believers are necessary to our spiritual growth. Sometimes they, just like Cheryl, have to get us "relocated" to a better place—like a nurturing church—where we won't be squashed by those hostile forces.

Birthing: trial. . .and triumph.

Shy

*"Do not be afraid, Abram.
I am your shield, your very great reward."*
GENESIS 15:1

Shy's name befits her. This gray-and-white cat with a rusty tint is timid and fearful of just about everything and everyone. When Don and his dad moved, Shy hid out in one of their living room chairs. Fortunately for the three of them, Don's dad was going to get rid of the old chair. He had to cut Shy out of the chair in order to get her out before setting the chair outside for trash pickup.

Augie, Don's dog, can sometimes get Shy to "box" with him, but the match is one sided. Shy, who has no claws, whaps Augie on the face and boxes his ears repeatedly. Augie keeps coming back for more. Shy doesn't hurt him. Augie humors her so that she can get some exercise.

A mouse recently got into the house, but Shy could not be depended on to catch him. She simply chased the mouse around the house. Don's dad had to be the one to capture the mouse and turn it loose outside.

Most people don't know that Don has a cat. She disappears as soon as company shows up at the door. Repeatedly startled in "fun" and teased as a kitten, Shy is now so skittish that she's almost invisible. Unlike Peter Pan, Shy would not miss her shadow if it ran away and hid from her.

Throughout the Bible the Lord God admonishes His people not to fear. In obedience to God, Abram had packed bag and baggage and moved to a distant land when he was seventy-five. For the next twenty-five years, Abram's life was in upheaval. He moved to Bethel. A famine forced him and his family to relocate to Egypt. He returned to Canaan and ended up going to war against neighboring kings. (See Genesis 12–14.) At the end of all this, God told Abram, "Do not be afraid" (Genesis 15:1).

As Moses faced a powerful enemy at Edrei, the "LORD said to Moses, 'Do not be afraid of him'" (Numbers 21:33–34). When Jairus heard that his daughter had died, Jesus said to him, "Don't be afraid" (Luke 8:50). When Paul and others were in the midst of a hurricane-force storm at sea, the Lord told him: "Do not be afraid, Paul" (Acts 27:24). The scriptures abound with the words *fear not* or *don't be afraid.*

There is One we are to fear. "I tell you, my friends,"

Jesus said, "do not be afraid of those who kill the body and after that can do no more. But I will show you whom you should fear: Fear him who, after your body has been killed, has authority to throw you into hell. Yes, I tell you, fear him" (Luke 12:4–5).

> Our God-fear can be tempered with comfort, for God is also compassionate.

Our God-fear can be tempered with comfort, for God is also compassionate. "The LORD has compassion on those who fear him" (Psalm 103:13). We need not be like fearful Shy. We can declare with the psalmist, "[The Lord] delivered me from all my fears" (34:4).

Calico

Catch for us the foxes, the little foxes that ruin the vineyards,
our vineyards that are in bloom.

SONG OF SONGS 2:15

Trent's new kitten, Calico, wanted to get in on the game. Trent was playing bocce ball with three other people. The balls used in this game are hard and heavy. The object is to get one's own colorful balls closest to the smaller target ball. It's like horseshoes without the horseshoes. Calico insisted on being a part of the game. Any one of the balls could seriously hurt her, but she insisted on chasing after them. One of the team players kept purposely missing the target in order to avoid bonking Calico on her not-so-smart noggin. No matter how many times Trent's dad moved Calico away from the yard game, she would come back. Fortunately, Calico never got beaned with one of the balls.

Some time later in the evening, when everyone was gathered around the bonfire, Trent noticed that Calico was gone. Everyone went on a search for the kitten, calling her name and looking for her. She had been constantly underfoot only a half hour earlier. Where could she have gone? Finally, Calico was found. She had been trapped under an upended small box beneath the picnic table.

Calico had missed getting hurt by a ball that could have done her serious injury, but something as inconsequential as a box may have imprisoned her for days or longer if everyone had not taken care to search for her until she was found.

Solomon didn't worry about big beasts coming in to ravage the vineyards belonging to him and his beloved, but "the little foxes." Jesus told His disciples not to fear those who could take their lives but to "be on your guard against the yeast of the Pharisees, which is hypocrisy." (See Luke 12:1, 4.) Jude warned against godless men who "have secretly slipped in among you. . .[and] who pervert the grace of our God into a license for immorality and deny Jesus Christ our only Sovereign and Lord" (Jude 4).

Those things that pose the greatest threat to scattering us as Christians worshipping and fellowshipping together are not the first things that may come to mind: persecution, death, or watching our church building go up in flames. Rather, the insidious things that sneak in among us are the things we need to guard against.

Being busybodies instead of simply busy is trouble in the making (2 Thessalonians 3:11). Being tolerant of teaching that does not line up doctrinally with the scriptures is to let little foxes into the vineyard (verse 14).

Distortion of the scriptures is another subtle trap

(1 Timothy 4:2–3). Like the Berean Christians, we need to examine "the Scriptures every day" (Acts 17:11) to make sure the little fox of error is not among us, destroying the vineyard. Our lives must be governed by "love" and by "true righteousness and holiness" (Ephesians 4:2, 24). Then, by "speaking the truth in love, we will grow to become in every respect the mature body of him who is the head, that is, Christ" (verse 15).

> Our lives must be governed by "love" and by "true righteousness and holiness" (Ephesians 4:2, 24).

Sandy

No temptation has overtaken you except
what is common to mankind.

1 Corinthians 10:13

There it was.

Hovering tantalizingly seven feet above where he sat on the floor.

Sandy, a fifteen-pound heavyweight, swished his tail back and forth in contemplation.

There are few things Sandy likes better in life than munching on his owner's bamboo plant. And there it loomed above him. Behind a collection of photographs, the green siren beckoned to him without a sound. Sandy walked around in front of the eighty-four-inch armoire once, then twice.

He gazed back up at the bamboo plant. He sat down. He swished his tail. Seven feet and several photographs between him and his favorite delicacy. He ran his pink tongue across his mouth. He flicked his whiskers. His ears twitched.

Hunching down, eyes fixed, withers ready, Sandy made his move. In one graceful quantum leap, Sandy cleared the distance between floor and armoire to land right in front of the irresistible bamboo plant. Success! He didn't so much as brush one of the precarious pictures poised in front of his precious plant.

"Sandy! Get down!"

Rats.

Caught again.

Betty says her cat Sandy must have "a spring in his sitter." In spite of his weight and the height of that plant, he has successfully scaled the armoire countless times—with never a miss or an askew photograph. When Betty leaves the house or goes to bed for the night, she never leaves her bamboo plant out. Even when she's at home during the day, however, Sandy sometimes risks life and limb (and getting caught) for just one taste of the tempting plant.

Those things that tempt us have that same allure. Temptations come in a variety of forms, each particularly suited for the one being tempted by the tempter. It is only the enemy of our souls who tempts us. "When tempted, no one should say, 'God is tempting me.' For God cannot be tempted by evil, nor does he tempt anyone" (James 1:13). James goes on to say that "each person is tempted when they are dragged away by their own evil desire and enticed" (verse 14).

Whatever tempts us, Jesus is able to help us through it. "Because he himself suffered when he was tempted, he is able to help those who are being tempted" (Hebrews 2:18). The writer of Hebrews sums it up beautifully: "For we do not have a high priest who is unable to empathize with our weaknesses, but we have one who has been tempted in every way, just as we are—yet he did not sin. Let us then approach God's throne of grace with confidence, so that we may receive mercy and find grace to help us in our time of need" (4:15–16).

> Whatever tempts us, Jesus is able to help us through it.

Like Betty standing guard to keep Sandy from eating himself sick on the tasty bamboo plant, the Lord won't let you "be tempted beyond what you can bear" (1 Corinthians 10:13). He stands ready to "provide a way out so that you can endure" (verse 13).

Dinky

*This man lived in the tombs. . . . He had often been chained
hand and foot, but he tore the chains apart
and broke the irons on his feet.*

MARK 5:3–4

*D*inky is a living oxymoron. Like Robin Hood's Little John, his name does not match his size. This eighteen-pound orange-and-white cat doesn't meow, either. He peeps. If these unusual traits aren't enough to make him stand out in a crowded room of kitties, there's his other idiosyncrasy. Dinky loves plastic grocery bags. He doesn't eat them; he licks them. But one day his plastic treat became fetters.

Dinky had become so engrossed in his licking ritual that he was completely inside a plastic bag. Unknowingly, he had scooted his bagged self to the table edge. Suddenly, Dinky and his bag tumbled off the table. Startled by his unforeseen free fall and sudden stop, Dinky whipped around to take off at a run. Unfortunately, one of the bag's handles looped around his neck.

Dinky found himself being pursued—and slowed down—by this monstrous, noisy white ghost hot on his heels. No matter where he ran, Dinky could not untangle himself from the bag that billowed out behind him like a space shuttle parachute.

Finally, Dinky's owner was able to come to his rescue in the basement. The bag hung in tatters but was still around the neck of the exhausted Dinky. Paul freed his wide-eyed, breathless, peepless Dinky from the plastic chains that still clung to him.

Filled with demons and terrorized mercilessly by them, the man lived among the tombs. Unlike the chains that could not hold him, the evil spirits held this man in their power. No matter where he roamed, no matter what he did, the demon-possessed man could not free himself from the demons that chained his mind and soul—until Jesus freed him (Mark 5:1–20). This account is also told in Luke. In a command full of love and power, Jesus tells the man who is now "dressed and in his right mind" (Luke 8:35), "Return home and tell how much God has done for you" (verse 39). With one word Jesus identifies Himself as who He is and how it is He has this kind of bondage-breaking power. He is God.

Dinky could not disentangle himself completely from his "chains" of plastic. The demon-possessed man could free himself from chains of iron, but he could not break free of the demonic shackles. There are some chains that only God can release us from or break. Fear, bitterness, anger, regret—from these chains the Lord Jesus Christ came to free us. "It is for freedom that Christ has set us free" (Galatians 5:1). "So if the Son sets you free," the Lord said, "you will be free indeed" (John 8:36). "Where the Spirit of the Lord is, there is freedom" (2 Corinthians 3:17).

> Jesus Christ is the great bondage breaker.

Jesus Christ is the great bondage breaker. As we come to Him, we can declare with the psalmist: "LORD. . .you have freed me from my chains" (Psalm 116:16).

Bibs

Wounds from a friend can be trusted,
but an enemy multiplies kisses.

PROVERBS 27:6

$\mathcal{I}$t was a standoff.

Aspen, the new cat in the household, stood across from Bibs. The hair on their backs and the growling emanating from deep in their chests told their owner, Jean, she had better separate the two and do it pronto. Making a wise decision, Jean decided to stop the fight before it started by dealing with her usually sweet-natured Bibs first. Making an unwise decision, Jean grabbed Bibs up and out of the impending cat fight.

Unleashing her "furry fury," as Jean called it in retrospect, Bibs bit Jean's hand deeply in several places. Jean was well acquainted with Bibs; she quickly washed her hand but thought little more of the incident.

Until the next day. And weeks subsequent to it.

After a trip to the hospital emergency department twenty-four hours later, Jean found her arm casted for three weeks to hold the surgically inserted drains in place. Because of the wounds she received from her "usually sweet-natured Bibs," Jean found herself making repeated trips to a hand surgeon over the course of the following weeks.

Neither Bibs nor Aspen received any injuries from their aborted fray, but Jean, like a slow-moving referee, had not escaped unscathed.

An amusing account in the book of Acts tells of some counterfeit exorcists who got in the middle of someone else's spiritual battle. They didn't end up in the emergency room, but they did have to run for their lives, wounded and naked (19:13–16).

The Lord speaks frequently of wounds in the Bible. Sometimes we are on the receiving end of wounds; sometimes we're on the giving end. Sometimes God must wound us; at other times we wound Him.

The well-meaning wounds or corrections of faithful friends and God can steer us in the right direction. "Blessed is the one whom God corrects," Job was told. God "wounds, but he also binds up," Eliphaz went on to

> **The well-meaning wounds or corrections of faithful friends and God can steer us in the right direction.**

say. "He injures, but his hands also heal" (Job 5:17–18). What Eliphaz said to his friend was true, but his timing only added undue, unnecessary pain. "The human spirit can endure in sickness, but a crushed spirit who can bear?" (Proverbs 18:14).

In the book of Jeremiah God says to His disobedient people, "Why do you cry out over your wound, your pain that has no cure? Because of your great guilt and many sins I have done these things to you" (30:15). Like those admonitions given by a true friend, God was out to turn His people around. Then He could go on to say, "But I will restore you to health and heal your wounds" (verse 17). Our faithful God knows when to wound us—and when to bind up our wounds. "By [Christ's] wounds we are healed" (Isaiah 53:5).

Unlike Bibs, who lashed out at the wrong person, our wounds from God serve to make us more like His Son. His promise to us is "I have wounded and I will heal" (Deuteronomy 32:39).

Frisky

For the Spirit God gave us does not make us timid,
but gives us power, love and self-discipline.

2 TIMOTHY 1:7

$\mathcal{F}$risky had a shaky start in life. With her calico coloring and pale green eyes, she is a striking animal whose coat is set off by the whiteness of her chest and paws. Frisky started off being just that—frisky.

Then Nikita entered the picture. A big Doberman with an attitude (he does not like cats), the peaceful house soon became a battlefield. Frisky would romp when Nikita was outside, but "lie low" was her motto when she was inside. Plans do go awry. . . .

Laura, Frisky's owner, heard a racket in the kitchen. She ran to see what it was. There was Frisky, pinned against the wall by Nikita. His big paws held Frisky fast, and the floor was red with. . .blood? Laura immediately stepped in, screaming at Nikita and reaching for her poor, terrorized cat. Although shaken, Frisky seemed uninjured. Much to Laura's relief, the red fluid all over the floor was not the blood of battle but red kidney bean juice. A jar had gotten broken in the fray. Laura decided the house wasn't big enough for both Nikita and Frisky.

Frisky was sent to a farm. What a transformation! Within weeks Frisky was as fat as she is long. No longer terrorized by Nikita, she was soon frisky again, her timidity forgotten. Frisky flattens her ears back and makes a full-bore run at the giant walnut tree. The tree acts as her tackling dummy. When she reaches it, she wraps all four legs around the base of the tree as far as she can.

That tree has been her inspiration. She flirts with all the other cats on the farm and is not at all intimidated by the other household animal—another Doberman. If Max the aging Doberman even looks at feisty Frisky, she gives him a look that says: *You don't want to mess with me. I've been besting a tree that's ten times your size. I come out the winner every time.*

Her intimidation tactic has worked. This Doberman doesn't mess with Frisky.

From Paul the apostle's letters to young pastor Timothy, we learn that Timothy wasn't an "in your face and in your space" kind of guy. In the verse above and throughout both books of Timothy, Paul is always encouraging his "son in the faith" to persevere in his ministry (see 1 Timothy 1:2). Several words of encouragement from Paul to Timothy we can use and apply in our own lives.

"Do not be ashamed of the testimony about our Lord" (2 Timothy 1:8).

"Be strong in the grace that is in Christ Jesus" (2:1).

"Join with me in suffering" (2:3).

Even Paul had to let go of his past failures. "Forgetting what is behind and straining toward what is ahead," he "press[ed] on" (Philippians 3:13–14).

> **Press on to what lies ahead.**

Don't allow past struggles to bind you. Like Frisky and Paul, forget what is behind. Press on to what lies ahead.

Miss Kitty

I can do all this through him who gives me strength.

PHILIPPIANS 4:13

She did not exactly show up on their doorstep. Young, shy, and injured, Miss Kitty came to Robin's house one day, seeking refuge under her porch. Robin had noticed that Miss Kitty never used one of her back legs, but until Robin held her for the first time, she didn't know why. Now she did. There was a festering hole there. Robin took Miss Kitty to the veterinarian.

Someone had shot Miss Kitty, the vet said. The wound was old. Now it was gangrenous. Miss Kitty's leg would have to be amputated at the hip. Miss Kitty had become a part of Robin's family now. She told the vet to proceed with the surgery.

Miss Kitty's recovery was long. With the gangrenous leg gone, however, and medication and TLC, Miss Kitty began to mend. She got better and soon got around very nicely on three legs.

Miss Kitty has mothered a number of healthy litters. She's an excellent mouser, too. One day Robin's son came running into the house, his eyes big with the excitement of discovery.

"Mom! Mom! Miss Kitty got a daddy mouse! He's on the back porch!"

Daddy mouse?

Robin went to investigate.

There, true to her son's word, lay a dead rat on her porch. And there stood three-legged Miss Kitty, proudly awaiting a reward for a job well done.

People and animals alike often overcome disabilities. Our great Creator has put some amazing "stuff" within our DNA. It's amazing stuff not only when we're healthy and whole, but also when we're not so whole or healthy. Some people will take the credit themselves, of course, but others have the wisdom and the humility to acknowledge their enabling God for His restorative

> Our great Creator has put some amazing "stuff" within our DNA.

grace. It may be physical prowess or emotional strength that comes by the hand of our loving Lord.

"I will repay [restore] you for the years the locusts have eaten," God told His emotionally battered and conquered people, Israel (Joel 2:25). Paul the apostle, who very likely had serious vision problems and whose body had been beaten countless times, could encourage his spiritual children to persevere based on his own experiences (Galatians 4:15; 6:17). He did not rail at God about his disabilities, whether congenitally acquired or inflicted by others. Paul saw them as one more reason to praise his Lord and Maker (2 Corinthians 12:9).

Darlene, a friend of mine who was born with only one hand, was overwhelmed when she brought her newborn daughter home from the hospital. There were no nurses around now to help her. Would she be able to manage all those "mommy things"?

"I can do this," she told herself determinedly.

Now she has three beautiful, growing daughters—the proof of God's enabling.

Three-legged Miss Kitty took out a very large, four-legged "daddy mouse." Be encouraged today that the Lord is able to perfect His power in our weakness (2 Corinthians 12:9). He is "able to do immeasurably more than all we ask or imagine" (Ephesians 3:20).

Sonny

[If] you have been trapped by what you said, ensnared by the
words of your mouth. . .go and humble yourself.

PROVERBS 6:2–3

Sonny likes to play a dangerous game. This orange-and-white cat makes his home with a family that includes three growing boys, a golden retriever, a python snake, and another cat, Tiger, who is getting up in years. Young Sonny, still in the prime of his life, is active and playful and. . .not too smart. He takes chances that Tiger, with years of experience to his credit, would never dream of.

Sonny's favorite game is to get Casey, the golden retriever, in a power play. Sonny antagonizes Casey and teases him, almost daring the big, gentle dog to do him harm. Sonny goes so far as to stick his head fully in Casey's mouth. But Casey, being the gentle dog that he is, never chomps down. Casey seems to understand that Sonny is just baiting him. If Casey ever "takes the bait," Sonny might find himself in a rather precarious position.

One day recently, Sonny got himself in a trap from which he could not escape. The family was gone for a long weekend. Sonny stayed close to home, but something in the backyard caught his fancy. He went over to investigate. Unknown to Sonny, the "something" was a lobster trap. Once again sticking his nose in where it didn't belong, Sonny got into a place he should have avoided. Only this time, the trap wasn't as obliging as Casey.

Sonny was trapped.

Solomon warned his son about being ensnared by his own words or unwise business dealings. He told him to take immediate action to rectify the error (Proverbs 6:1–5). The Lord Jesus Christ warned us about wanton or preoccupied lifestyles in light of His approaching return. "Be careful, or your hearts will be weighed down with carousing, drunkenness and the anxieties of life, and that day will close on you suddenly like a trap" (Luke 21:34). Paul told his spiritual son Timothy that the desire for influence and the desire for wealth are traps to be avoided (1 Timothy 3:6; 6:9).

Traps may be of our own making or someone else's. Like Sonny with Casey, we may be able to escape unscathed. At other times we may need help. Or we may need to free someone else from a snare as Sonny was freed from the lobster trap. Powerless against unseen snares, we, too, have a resource. We can call on God as David did. "Keep me safe from the traps set by evildoers" (Psalm 141:9).

In these days of terror strikes and sinister plots, we have One we can call on for help. We can pray for our country's leaders and our dear ones with the words of Israel's historic leader, David, who often found himself beset by enemies on all sides. He took appropriate measures as we must, too (see 2 Samuel 5, 7–8). Also, like David, we can pray, "Keep me safe, LORD, from the hands of the wicked; protect me from the violent, who devise ways to trip my feet" (Psalm 140:4).

> In these days of terror strikes and sinister plots, we have One we can call on for help.

Lacey

"For what mortal has ever heard the voice of the living God speaking out of fire, as we have, and survived?"

DEUTERONOMY 5:26

Lacey is a survivor. This beautiful Siamese cat is headstrong and fiercely independent, convinced she can take on any challenge. It may have all started when she was just a few years old and got locked in a church fellowship hall for two weeks.

Rachel looked everywhere for her cat. Like other people whose cats turn up missing, Rachel put up posters and signs with her telephone number and Lacey's picture. No one responded. Rachel asked a woman who attended the church behind their house if they had seen a cat around. No one had. Finally, Rachel's dad went on a search mission. That's when he found Lacey, locked up in the church reception hall. Lacey had survived on a water diet, but she didn't get her water from any faucet or bowl. . . .

From that point on Lacey has been a survivor. She doesn't back down from any dogs; she beats them up. Lacey opens the house's sliding glass door by herself, though she never takes the time to close it. She has the most varied diet of any feline on the planet, but her personal favorites are dog food, peanut butter sandwiches, and vegetables.

Lacey is, as I said, a survivor. But you'd never know it to see her sitting primly on the kitchen stool, awaiting her peanut butter breakfast.

As Moses stood before his people after the giving of the Ten Commandments, he reiterated to them some key points. He was the one who went up the mountain to receive the Law from the Lord God. They "were afraid of the fire and did not go up the mountain" (Deuteronomy 5:5). Although the people feared they would not be able to survive in the presence of the One who spoke out of the fire, their survival depended on this One of whom they were rightfully in awe. "Oh," the Lord said, "that their hearts would be inclined to fear me and keep all my commands always, *so that it might go well with them and their children forever!*" (verse 29, emphasis added). To be careful to walk in the way "the LORD. . .has commanded" is to "prosper and prolong" our days (verse 33). It is how we truly survive.

As I pen these words, a variety of "survival" programs are popular on network television. Usually, cases of surviving against all odds occur when there are no cameras around to videotape the event for posterity. True survival in difficult times is hardly entertainment. We can ask the downed pilot who summons all his resources to survive in enemy territory, or missionaries miles from medical help when their child is desperately ill. As for them, as it was for the Israelites with Moses, survival is not in keeping our distance from God, but in finding "the favor of him who dwelt in the burning bush" (Deuteronomy 33:16).

> Sometimes survival is not to be fit but to submit.

Sometimes survival is not to be fit but to submit.

Candy

I have been in danger from. . .bandits,
in danger from my fellow Jews, in danger from Gentiles. . .
and in danger from false believers.

2 CORINTHIANS 11:26

With black face and paws and sky-blue eyes, Candy is a beautiful Himalayan cat with striking Siamese seal point markings. Candy is beautiful to look at and a daytime playmate for Jackie. With unusual equanimity for a cat, Candy allows her young owner all kinds of liberties. Jackie loves to dress Candy up like a baby doll. Candy even stays in the baby doll high chair all dressed up in her baby doll regalia. Candy endures all sorts of humiliation and discomfort throughout the day, looking every bit like a true friend to Jackie.

Then Jackie goes to bed for the night.

As soon as Jackie falls asleep with her favorite toy clutched to her chest, Candy leaps up on Jackie's bed with practiced stealth. She pulls Sugar Bear out of Jackie's arms and steals away with the precious toy. Candy also takes advantage of the cover of night to steal something else from Jackie—her Barbie doll accessories. With all the cunning of her kind, Candy stashes them in the last place anyone would think to look—the dog's bed. (It was months before Jackie's mother found them there for the first time.)

When Candy finishes her night's marauding, she claims Barbie's camper as her bed. Candy is not the true friend she appears to be. Her companionable trustworthiness is a daytime illusion.

Some of our most difficult interpersonal challenges in life have to do with people who we think are fellow Christians. These are folks we depend on in a crisis, turn to for advice, and admire for their virtue. Then we learn we've been deceived.

We discover our pastor has been "on the take" for years.

We find out that an elder from church has dealt with others—and us—dishonestly in repeated business transactions.

Our child's Sunday school teacher plans a class party with a Ouija board as one of the evening's "games."

It is hard to rectify any of these situations with people who claim Jesus Christ as their Lord and Savior. When Paul listed the groups of people he had been in danger from in the text above, it's likely that his greatest suffering came from those who were not what they appeared to be—those he called "false believers" (2 Corinthians 11:26). Jude said, "Certain individuals. . .have secretly slipped in among you. They are ungodly people, who pervert the grace of our God into a license for immorality and deny Jesus Christ our only Sovereign and Lord" (Jude 4).

In these days of charlatans and those who have "a form of godliness but [deny] its power" (2 Timothy 3:5), we need to be wary. The Lord Jesus Christ said, "By their fruit you will recognize them" (Matthew 7:16). A purloining, friendly feline warrants a smile—a false brother, judgment. We need to heed the words of the Lord Jesus and "be as shrewd as snakes and as innocent as doves" (10:16).

> **We need to heed the words of the Lord Jesus and "be as shrewd as snakes and as innocent as doves."**

Spotty

"The LORD is a warrior; the LORD is his name."

EXODUS 15:3

Robert, Henry, Stephen, Mark, and Rebekah are four brothers and a sister who live in Burkina Faso, Africa. As children of missionary parents, they live an interesting and unusual life when compared with most American children. Like many of their counterparts here in the USA, however, the boys and their sister have a pet. He is a young white cat with black spots. Spotty is his name.

Like most cats in Burkina, Spotty is small. But what he lacks in size he makes up for in sinewy strength and stealth. Spotty is a superior warrior. He can be depended on to fight off and overpower enemies that are common where Rebekah and her brothers call home. To his credit Spotty has killed at least three snakes. One of those snakes was a spitting cobra; the other two were poisonous green mambas. Spotty is also a rat killer. He has killed numerous rats, one of them twice his size. All the reward Spotty expects is a pat on the head and some words of praise. Accordingly, Spotty deposits his spoils of war on the back porch.

A dead rat would not be a particularly welcoming sight early in the morning. . .but it beats starting the day with a live one sitting on the back porch.

God, who is all-powerful, gives amazing strength to unlikely warriors. When young David told King Saul he would do battle against Goliath, Saul rebuked him. "You are only a young man, and he has been a warrior from his youth" (1 Samuel 17:33). Yet it was David who walked away the victor (verse 50).

When Nehemiah was leading the rebuilding of the walls of Jerusalem, he didn't feel strong enough for the task. His enemies gloated to that effect. "Their hands will get too weak for the work," they said, "and it will not be completed." But Nehemiah prayed four simple words: "Now strengthen my hands" (Nehemiah 6:9), and "the wall was completed. . . . When all our enemies heard about this, all the surrounding nations were afraid and lost their self-confidence, because they realized that this work had been done with the help of our God" (verses 15–16). God can give the strength to do the improbable and even what may seem to be impossible.

> God can give the strength to do the improbable and even what may seem to be impossible.

In tender words to the church in Philadelphia, Christ says, "I know that you have little strength" (Revelation

3:8). Christ did not ask them to do anything great or impressive. Rather, He said, "Hold on to what you have" (verse 11). Sometimes our greatest show of strength is to simply hold on to what we have.

We may not be up against poisonous green mambas or dog-sized rats like Spotty is. We may not have to battle a seasoned warrior. But in the tasks that demand strength of body, spirit, or will, we can call on David's God. We can ask for help from Nehemiah's enabler. We can turn to the Creator who empowers a little cat to destroy dangerous predators.

"The Lord is faithful, and he will strengthen and protect you from the evil one" (2 Thessalonians 3:3).

Mama Cat

How could one man chase a thousand, or two put ten thousand
to flight, unless their Rock had sold them,
unless the LORD had given them up?

DEUTERONOMY 32:30

Mama Cat lived up to her name. In her twenty-one years of life, she had litter after litter of kittens. Every spring and fall, like clockwork, Mama Cat had a new litter. Good homes were always found for each of her kittens, too. Mama Cat's mothering instincts were so ingrained that she enjoyed seeing the puppies of Suzy and Fluffy, the two dogs next door. She in turn would invite Suzy and Fluffy in to show off her litters. But Mama Cat had a dark side when it came to bulldogs.

She hated the bulldog who lived in the house on the other side of her. If Georgie came out and saw Mama Cat, he couldn't get back in his house fast enough. He was deathly afraid of Mama Cat. Not only did Mama Cat hate Georgie the Bulldog next door; she hated all bulldogs.

As Mama Cat lounged contentedly in the front yard one summer day, a little boy came up the street with his dog. The little boy and his dog were total strangers to

Mama Cat, but that made no difference. The stranger's dog was not a Pomeranian like Fluffy, nor a big black-and-white mix like Suzy. He was a bulldog. Fast as a flash, Mama Cat jumped up and leaped onto the bulldog's back. She rode him halfway down the street, dog barking and little boy yelling all the way.

She waltzed back to her own front yard as pretty as you please and settled in for the rest of her afternoon sunbathing. That little boy and his bulldog never went by Mama Cat's house again.

In the days of Gideon, Israel was surrounded by hostile enemies. Gideon was least likely to lead his people to victory—which he quickly pointed out to the Lord (Judges 6:15). But God told him, "I will be with you, and you will strike down all the Midianites" (verse 16). When the time for battle came, the Lord determined that no one would ever doubt that the victory was His. Gideon and 300 Israelites defeated 135,000 Midianites (8:4–12).

Someone coined the phrase "One man plus God is a majority." This may be a loose paraphrase of the verse from Deuteronomy above, or from God's promise to His people for obedience. "Five of you will chase a hundred, and a hundred of you will chase ten thousand, and your enemies will fall by the sword before you" (Leviticus 26:8). God's mathematics are mind boggling.

The Lord God demonstrates His unique mathematics in His Son, too. Though we are all sinners by inheritance and by choice (Romans 5:19; Ecclesiastes 7:20), "through the obedience of the one man [Christ Jesus] the many will be made righteous" (Romans 5:19).

One lone cat terrorized any bulldog in her path. How much more we can accomplish when, like Gideon with the Lord God, we become a majority.

> **How much more we can accomplish when, like Gideon with the Lord God, we become a majority.**

Moe

Fight the good fight of the faith.

1 TIMOTHY 6:12

Moe had done it time and time again. He was a roamer and a fighter. He came home to eat and sometimes to sleep, but he was a scrapper by nature, and there was nothing he liked better than being a brawler. But this time was different than the others.

Joyce came home to find her black, feisty fighter lying in a heap on her back porch. Whomever or whatever he had fought with this time had apparently been the victor. Moe had never been so injured that he could not walk into the house. Joyce would have to put all her nursing skills to work to repair the damage.

Most of Moe's injuries were the usual variety: missing tufts of fur, scratches, small lacerations. This time, however, he had a gaping wound that stretched from the corner of his mouth down to his shoulder. Unable to afford a trip to the veterinary clinic, Joyce decided to close the wound herself. With the assistance of her daughter, some medications, and a suture kit, Joyce was able to suture Moe's gash. With regular application of antibiotic ointment, the wound healed beautifully. Moe made a full recovery.

However, neither Moe's wounds nor his mending changed his ways. He went back to his usual skirmishes within days. He still comes home with cuts, scratches, and bald spots, but he's more selective when it comes to picking fights now. Evidently, Moe is determined to "claw his way to the top," but with a bit more discernment.

Nevertheless, he's still a roamer. He's still a scrapper. And he's still a fighter.

Some people spend their lives fighting—sometimes the wrong thing or person.

Saul spent months, if not years, fighting against the God whom he claimed to serve. The resurrected Lord Jesus stopped him while he "was still breathing out murderous threats against the Lord's disciples" (Acts 9:1). When Christ accosted him, He said to Saul, "Saul, Saul, why do you persecute me? It is hard for you to kick against the goads" (26:14). Like beasts of burden resisting the goads used to prod them along, so Jesus told Saul it was painful for him to resist Him. It may be that Saul had a niggling suspicion that his persecution of believers was in error.

Saul's fight against the Lord God ended that day, but not his fighting days. "I do not fight like a boxer beating the air," he said later. "No, I strike a blow to my body and make it my slave" (1 Corinthians 9:26–27). His goal was to be a man of the Spirit and not of the flesh.

Saul the street fighter became Paul the spiritual boxer. Like Paul we, too, should battle against what is evil and "fight the good fight of the faith" (1 Timothy 6:12). We may get beaten up along the way, but at the end of our life here on earth, we will be able to say with Paul, "I have fought the good fight. . .I have kept the faith" (2 Timothy 4:7).

> Like Paul we, too, should battle against what is evil and "fight the good fight of the faith" (1 Timothy 6:12).

Mia

To whom can I speak and give warning?
Who will listen to me?

<small>JEREMIAH 6:10</small>

Mia's full-throated, rumbling growl came menacingly from deep within her chest.

Christine looked up from the sofa where she lay recovering from surgery she'd had earlier that week. She had never seen her docile, tortoiseshell calico carry on in such a way. Puzzled, she called to Mia to come. Like a watchman on a tower, Mia did not move from the front door of the apartment. She ignored Christine and continued to growl. All over her body, Mia's hair stood up on end. Her ears were back. Her entire body was taut with readiness.

Then a knock sounded on the door.

Mia stood her ground, still growling. Christine got up and went to the door but did not open it. Her apartment door had no peephole. She wasn't expecting anyone, and she was home alone.

"Who is it?"

"Gas. I was called to check the gas."

Christine hadn't called anyone. She didn't know of any

problem. Maybe her husband had called about something?

Mia continued her low growl. She didn't move from her place on the floor beside Christine. Christine looked at Mia again. Her cat had never acted this way before.

"You'd better check with the landlord first," she said to the male voice on the other side of the door.

She heard footsteps echo down the hall as the uninvited "utility man" walked away.

Christine returned to the sofa. Mia stood at the door a second longer and returned to plop herself down next to Christine. Her fur had lost its electrically charged appearance. Her ears were in their usual perky position. She purred contentedly.

No utility inspector had been summoned to Christine's apartment complex that day. And Mia never acted that way again.

Warnings come in a variety of ways. A hand signal, a barking dog, a wailing siren, an activated security light—all can warn us of impending danger. God issues warnings as well. Throughout the Bible He warns of punishment for sin and disobedience. He spoke warnings through prophets like Ezekiel (Ezekiel 3:16–21). Paul told the Ephesian church elders, "Remember that for three years I never stopped warning each of you night and day with tears" to be on guard against false brothers (Acts 20:31). Many crucial historical events "were written down as warnings for us" (1 Corinthians 10:11).

Like Christine heeding her cat's warning, we need to heed the words of warning the Lord God has given us. "See to it that you do not refuse him who speaks. If they [the Israelites with Moses at Mount Sinai] did not escape when they refused him who warned them on earth, how much less will we, if we turn away from him who warns us from heaven?" (Hebrews 12:25).

> **Obedience to God's ordinances brings double blessing.**

Our instructions and warnings for living life God's way are clearly given in the Bible. Obedience to God's ordinances brings double blessing. "By them your servant is warned; in keeping them there is great reward" (Psalm 19:11).

Day by Day and Step-by-Step

*Prowling his own quiet backyard
or asleep by the fire, he is still only
a whisker away from the wilds.*

JEAN BURDEN

Freckles

And pray for us, too, that God may open a door for our message, so that we may proclaim the mystery of Christ, for which I am in chains.

COLOSSIANS 4:3

Thumpity-thumpity-thumpity-thumpity. . .
Thud!
Zzzzzzzzzzzzzzzzzzzzzzzzzzzzzp!
Whump!

Twenty pounds of striped orange tabby with freckles on his face zipping by effortlessly. Meet Freckles. Freckles has perfected his own unique way of getting a carnival-like ride through the house. He begins his amusement park ride by running through every room of the house. *Thumpity-thumpity-thumpity-thumpity.* As he gallops on the hardwood floors, the echo of his paws on the flooring resonates throughout the house. Then he lands on his favorite throw rug. *Thud!* On the last leg of his wild ride he stands gloating. He sails across the final stretch on his throw rug, fur streaming back from his freckled face. *Zzzzzzzzzzzzzzzzzzzzzzzzzzzzzp!* He comes to a slow stop just as he lightly hits the kitchen door. *Whump!*

Freckles gets up and sashays away. Another successful,

stimulating slide ride across the floorboards! Every day his pattern never changes.

Thumpity-thumpity-thumpity-thumpity!

Thud!

Zzzzzzzzzzzzzzzzzzzzzzzzzzzzp!

Whump!

Exhilarating. Pure, unadulterated, unacademic, unpretentious fun. Every day. What could go wrong?

Thumpity-thumpity-thumpity-thumpity. . .

Thud!

Zzzzzzzzzzzzzzzzzzzzzzzzzzzzp!

Who left the kitchen door open?

Freckles went flying out the kitchen door, rug and all—across the porch, down the steps, onto the grass. He left a little yellow trail behind him all the way. . . .

> Only one door is a sure thing: the door named Jesus Christ.

Sid, a physician, was intently reading over a chart as he began his exit. The automatic detector for the sliding glass door failed in its automatic function.

Whump! Sid hit the door head-on.

Only one door is a sure thing: the door named Jesus Christ. If by Him anyone enters, "he shall be saved" (John 10:9 KJV).

There are other doors of ministry once we're saved.

Sometimes God opens them; sometimes He closes them. When the door closed on Paul to do any ministry in the Corinthian synagogue, he "went next door to the house of Titius Justus" (Acts 18:7). There he had a favorable and fruitful response to his message. A "great door for effective work" opened for him in Ephesus, but not everyone had opened the door of their heart to the Gospel (1 Corinthians 16:9). The "Lord had opened a door" for Paul in Troas, but he did not stay. He was anxious to find his friend Titus. He took advantage of the open door but not for long (2 Corinthians 2:12–13).

Like Freckles, we may assume a door is shut—only to find the open door of someone with a heart ready to hear the Gospel. At other times we assume we have a wide-open door for ministry. Then we find ourselves running into it. Those in outreach evangelism never know if doors will be slammed in their faces or flung open with eager joy. It is, as a friend of mine likes to say, simply "one of those God things."

Anticipate walking through some doors of ministry today? Like Paul, garner some prayer support first. It may save you from sliding into more than you bargained for—or banging your head accidentally.

George

"Why will you die, people of Israel? For I take no pleasure in the death of anyone, declares the Sovereign LORD. Repent and live!"

EZEKIEL 18:31–32

*A*lexis came running up to her mother, her eyes big with fear and her voice quavering.

"I saw his paws! And then he was gone!"

Chris went to investigate. Their cat, Fatboy George, has a bad habit. As he looks out at the day from his perch inside the open window, he's not able to resist the call of the outdoors. George nibbles on the safety tabs that hold the screen securely in the frame. Then he wedges his pudgy body out and around the second-story screen to sit himself down in the flower box. There! A perfect spot from which to enjoy the day.

Chris went to the bedroom window with young Alexis. Sure enough, the screen had been pushed loose, but there was no George. Fearing the worst, she gave Alexis strict instructions.

"You stay here. Mommy will go check on George."

Chris ran back down the steps and outside. There sat George: stunned but uninjured. George chose to break the ground rules. He learned the hard way that the ground. . .rules.

Just as loving parents do for their children, or caring pet owners do for their pets, the Lord God Almighty has established ground rules and boundaries for us as well. His rules are neither arbitrary nor fatuous but intended for our good.

Ezekiel the prophet pled with his people who were in captivity not to repeat the mistakes of their ancestors. Through him God warned the Israelites to repent. "Turn away from all your offenses," they were told, "then sin will not be your downfall" (Ezekiel 18:30). Centuries before, Moses gave a similar admonition. "I have set before you life and death, blessings and curses. Now choose life that you and your children may live" (Deuteronomy 30:19). Centuries after Israel's captivity in Babylon, the message has not changed. "Repent, then, and turn to God, so that your sins may be wiped out" (Acts 3:19).

God's boundaries are clearly laid out in His Word, the Bible. He has put obstacles—tabs on the screens, if you will—to keep us safe. He is out to protect us from injuring ourselves or others. Sometimes His rules are precise. "You shall not commit adultery"; "You shall not murder" (James 2:11; Exodus 20:13–14). Sometimes His

> **God's boundaries are clearly laid out in His Word, the Bible.**

boundaries are subtler. "Do not judge, or you too will be judged" (Matthew 7:1). "You, then, who teach others, do you not teach yourself?" (Romans 2:21). Occasionally He whispers counsel to us through His Holy Spirit (John 14:26) or through the sage advice of friends (Proverbs 27:9).

Like George, we may land on our feet when we have transgressed a boundary. Then again, we may not. Our "stunning" may set us back a few steps on our way to becoming like Christ. God, our loving protector, will come to our aid as Chris did for George. But how much better to avoid the tantalizing but unsafe window box for the safe haven of obedience.

Snowball and Muffin

*Then the LORD said to him [Moses],
"What is that in your hand?"*

EXODUS 4:2

Snowball moved in with Barb when her previous owners no longer wanted to take care of her. Snowy white from nose to tail, this domestic short-haired cat has no real claim to fame. She doesn't do anything out of the ordinary or have any unusual characteristics, but she knows what to do with what's available to her.

When Barb received a gift of some good-sized jingle bells for Christmas, she hung the colorful ribbon with its bells on her front doorknob. Several days later Barb heard the bells ringing. She went to the door and found Snowball hitting the bells with her paw. The Christmas bells never got put away once the New Year rang in. They became Snowball's regular way of saying, "Time to go out!"

Muffin is just the opposite of Snowball. Black from her ears to her toenails, she has a very unusual talent. Muffin's owner, Lois, bought a toy play piano complete with instructional phase lights for her daughters. Imagine her surprise when she heard "Jingle Bells" being played flawlessly. Lois went to investigate which one of her daughters was the budding concert pianist.

To her surprise, there was Muffin, watching the piano lights before her. She precisely placed a paw on the keys necessary to render a faultless rendition of "Jingle Bells." And, like Snowball, Muffin puts her paw to work jingling bells whenever it suits her. It doesn't have to be Christmas.

Both Snowball and Muffin use what they have at hand to jingle bells—their paws.

When God called Moses to lead the Israelites out of their years of bondage in Egypt, Moses was hesitant to undertake such an awesome responsibility. When God asked him what he had in his hand, Moses replied, "A staff." God commanded him to throw it on the ground. Doing so, Moses then ran from the snake that had been his staff. He couldn't run far; God commanded him to pick the snake up (by the tail, no less). The snake once again became Moses' staff (Exodus 3:7–4:4). When Moses protested that he wasn't a motivational speaker, God asked him, "Who gave human beings their mouths? . . . Is it not I, the LORD?" (4:10–11). God expects us to use what we have available to us. He proved to Moses that no matter how little or much we have, He is the enabler.

When the Lord Jesus Christ sent out seventy-two of His followers to announce, "The kingdom of God has come near to you" (Luke 10:9), He empowered them with the ability to heal the sick and exorcise demons. These men were given no other supplies. They were instructed not to so much as pack a bag or take extra cash (10:1–20). They were to use what they had at hand—their hands, their feet, their mouths. Just like Moses.

> The Lord God marvelously enables us to do what He commands.

The Lord God marvelously enables us to do what He commands. He doesn't want excuses. He wants obedience.

Meow Kitty

You. . .must teach what is appropriate to sound doctrine.

Titus 2:1

Meow Kitty had a conspicuous beginning in his second home. One balmy spring day, all of Barb's other cats were acting peculiarly. Their strange behavior was traced to Meow Kitty. Having been abandoned, this white, long-haired feline had torn a hole in Barb's kitchen screen door. He then jumped up on the counter, positioning himself squarely on his own bully pulpit. He was ready to begin Lesson One for the other curious cats, peering up at him wonderingly from their places on the floor. Barb didn't want her cats being taught those kinds of tricks, so she gave Meow Kitty to June.

Meow Kitty is a teacher by nature. When June added a new basset hound puppy to the household, Meow Kitty immediately stepped in as Honey's mentor and teacher. He showed Honey where the food and water were. He taught Honey how to get her short little legs up the stairs. Not convinced that this new member of the family knew how to keep herself properly groomed and cleaned, Meow Kitty washed her. Honey is so accustomed to learning from and following her teacher that sometimes Meow Kitty can't get rid of her. Honey dogs his every step. Meow Kitty has done such a thorough job educating and teaching Honey the proverbial "ropes" that Honey doesn't really know she is a dog.

Honey turns up her nose at dog doodles. Like her teacher, Honey only plays with catnip toys.

All of us are teachers at one time or another—whether we want to be or not. As we learn from others by instruction or observation, so we, too, teach others. The Bible is filled with instruction for teachers. The book of Titus is replete with the word *teach*. Although Paul, the book's writer, starts off with a warning about those who are "teaching things they ought not to teach" (1:11), he quickly changes his focus to what should be taught.

> **All of us are teachers at one time or another—whether we want to be or not.**

"Teach the older men to be temperate, worthy of respect, self-controlled, and sound in faith, in love and in endurance," he says (2:2). Older women are to be taught to be "reverent in the way they live" and "to teach what is good" themselves (verse 3). All the teaching that we or others do is summed up in what God's grace teaches us. "It teaches us to say 'No' to ungodliness and worldly passions, and to live self-controlled, upright and godly lives" (verse 12).

We may have days when we feel like a mature cat trying to teach a young puppy the way of the household. Or maybe we are like the puppy—cutting our teeth on catnip. Either way, the lessons of life abound around us. Our perfect Teacher, the Holy Spirit, will never teach us error. As the Lord Jesus Christ promised, "The Holy Spirit, whom the Father will send in my name, will teach you all things" (John 14:26).

There's no Teacher like God Himself!

Tigger

"Martha, Martha," the Lord answered,
"you are worried and upset about many things,
but few things are needed—or indeed only one."

Luke 10:41–42

What is it about cats that they like to deliver their kittens in the beds of little boys? Chris had taken care to prepare a nice box for Tigger, her family's butterscotch-colored cat, to deliver her kittens in. Tigger usually slept in the boys' room, so that's where Chris put the box turned bed. She took pains to make it cozy and comfortable for Tigger and her brood-to-be. All to be done now was to await the day of delivery.

A shriek shattered the early Saturday morning silence. Startled from sleep, Chris ran to her boys' room. Young Jacob was pointing to the foot of his bed.

"Look!"

There at the foot of the bed, on top of Jacob's covers, was Tigger. She was nestled snuggly next to Molly, the family's border collie mix. So was Tigger's new litter of kittens. Mother cat, baby kittens, and Aunt Molly the dog were huddled together in a happy heap.

The Purrfect Puddy Tat Delivery Bed sat empty and unused on the floor, right next to Jacob's bed. Chris yawned and waved off her son's big eyes.

"They'll be fine," she told her son. "We'll deal with it later."

Chris regarded the furry brood once more. *Cute.*

She yawned again. She closed the door. And she promptly went back to bed.

Martha and her sister, Mary, are a study in contrasts. Mary, sitting at the feet of Jesus, was oblivious to "all the preparations that had to be made." Martha was not just busy with those preparations; she was "distracted" by them (Luke 10:39–40). The Greek word means to be drawn "in different ways at the same time." While Mary was mesmerized by the Lord, Martha felt like she was being drawn and quartered. "Don't you care," she asked the Lord, "that my sister has left me to do the work by myself?" She did not give the Lord a chance to answer. "Tell her to help me!" (verse 40).

Ever so kindly, the Lord told Martha that only one thing was needed. Mary had "chosen what is better." He would not take that from her (verse 42)—and neither should Martha. He did not say that Martha's preparations were wrong. He did say there was something better to attend to.

Every day is filled with "many things" that worry and

upset us. The office report must be completed. Company is coming and the house is dirty. Our homework still isn't done. It's our only morning of the week to sleep in, and the cat births her kittens in someone else's bed. With all that and more, the Lord still expects us to give ourselves to the "one thing that is needed."

Christ Himself is the one thing that is needed above all else. Make time today to sit "at the Lord's feet listening to what he [says]" (verse 39).

> **Christ Himself is the one thing that is needed above all else.**

Callie

Let your eyes look straight ahead; fix your gaze directly before you. . . . Do not turn to the right or the left; keep your foot from evil.

PROVERBS 4:25, 27

Callie steadfastly gazes at the door until Penny comes home from work. This black-as-midnight cat consistently meets and greets her owner at the door every day without fail. When Penny makes the long trip from northwest Ohio to Pennsylvania to visit her family, Callie rides along in the car, contentedly gazing out the window. She knows what's ahead, especially in the spring and summer.

As soon as they arrive "home," Callie scampers to her place among the pink impatiens. Her black head providing a stark contrast, she plants herself carefully among the flowers, never so much as bending or breaking a single one of them. Once she has settled in, she gazes at her surroundings, eagerly awaiting birds, bugs, squirrels, or chipmunks to cross her path. Then, of course, the chase is on. But until that time, she is content to take in everything at her leisure—including a satisfying drink of water from the birdbath.

Sometimes Callie gazes in intense concentration for a purpose. Sometimes her lingering stare is simply for the pure pleasure of it. Either way, her gaze is riveted on the subject at hand.

Premature infants are fascinating, precious people. But because they are born early, they are not ready to assimilate the myriad of sounds, sights, and sensations that assault them as they arrive prematurely into this blinding, cold, noisy world from their quiet, dark, warm, fluid environment. They have a number of unique ways to minimize this sensory overload, but often they cannot. For "preemies" a locked gaze often indicates an inability to cope with or adapt to their environment. The infant becomes fixated on an object that won't let him or her go. The baby has to be gently nurtured back to a state of repose.

> **There are things we should gaze upon—and other things we need to avoid locking on to.**

There are things we should gaze upon—and other things we need to avoid locking on to. The psalmist said he desired to "gaze on the beauty of the LORD" (Psalm 27:4). Elihu instructed Job and his friends to "gaze at the clouds so high above" (Job 35:5) and contemplate God's righteousness. These are worthy of our concentration.

Yet we are warned against gazing upon the wrong

things, too. "Do not gaze at wine when it is red," we're instructed, "when it sparkles in the cup, when it goes down smoothly!" (Proverbs 23:31). Job may have needed to look up and gaze, but when it is time for action, quiet contemplation must cease.

After the disciples watched Christ ascend to heaven, they remained gaping at the scene. Two angels came alongside them and said, "Why stand ye gazing up into heaven?" (Acts 1:11 KJV). It was time to get going, spreading the good news of the resurrected Savior!

The Bible speaks of "fixing our eyes on Jesus" (Hebrews 12:2). With proper focus we, too, can do the kingdom's work. For "our salvation is nearer now than when we first believed" (Romans 13:11).

Chocolate

*Then Jesus told his disciples a parable to show them
that they should always pray and not give up.*

LUKE 18:1

When early morning comes, Chocolate doesn't like to be kept waiting for his breakfast. This black cat has adopted Martha's work schedule as his breakfast schedule. When 4:45 a.m. rolls around, Chocolate is literally in Martha's face (whether she has to get up for work or not) to awaken her.

Chocolate is very methodical with his early morning wake-up call. He begins with the gentle approach. Gently placing his paw on Martha's face, he pats her cheek repeatedly to tell her he's hungry. If Martha burrows her head under her pillow or manages to sleep through the pat-pat-pat on her cheek, Chocolate goes to plan B. He puts constant pressure on Martha's arm as a way to rouse her. Claws are never extended. Chocolate simply bears down with one padded front paw. There are days that method fails, too. Chocolate goes to plan C.

This persistent black cat has learned to operate Martha's alarm clock. He surreptitiously walks over to the nightstand and begins pushing the buttons on top of the clock. He invariably gets the combination right.

Bzzzzt-bzzzzt-bzzzzt. . .

Martha is up. Chocolate runs his tongue over the smirk on his whiskered face.

Breakfast!

The Lord Jesus Christ, God incarnate, was a Man of prayer. After a full day of preaching, He prayed all night until at least three o'clock in the morning (Mark 6:46–48). Before choosing the twelve men who would learn from Him and work alongside Him for His three years of ministry, He spent the night in prayer (Luke 6:12–13). Jesus illustrated in practice what He taught by words in regard to prayerful persistence.

In the parable of the unjust judge and the wronged widow, Jesus said the widow kept badgering the indifferent judge. "For some time he refused," Jesus said. "But finally he said to himself, 'Even though I don't fear God or care what people think, yet because this widow keeps bothering me, I will see that she gets justice, so that she won't eventually come and attack me!' " (Luke 18:4–5). Even a calloused judge can be "worn down" to do the right thing.

Christ went on to say our heavenly Father is not like that. He will "bring about justice for his chosen ones. . . . He will see that they get justice, and quickly" (verses 7–8). Isn't that a wonderful truth to know? God does not need to be badgered or pestered by us for Him to answer our prayers.

Yet God wants to develop in us a persistent, prayerful spirit. In terms of time, do we pursue God in prayer as relentlessly as we do our stockbroker or physician? The words replaced by the ellipsis in the quote above read: "And will not God bring about justice for his chosen ones, who cry out to him day and night?" (verse 7). Are we like Chocolate, persisting until the answer comes?

> God does not need to be badgered or pestered by us for Him to answer our prayers.

Christ persisted in prayer. We cannot do less. "Pray continually" (1 Thessalonians 5:17).

Kiki

*And without faith it is impossible to please God, because
anyone who comes to him must believe that he exists and that
he rewards those who earnestly seek him.*

Hebrews 11:6

Kiki is the consummate hunter. Being a city cat has in no
way hampered her hunting prowess or stopped her from
stalking her various victims. Not far from the house where
she lives is a woods, so she doesn't realize that her hunting
ground is fairly restricted. Kiki loves the word *impossible.*
She proves it in her practiced hunting and with the prey
she brings home for "show-and-tell."

This calico cat is not one to waste her time on mice and
bugs. She is a big-game hunter. She hunts rabbits that are
twice her size. Kiki doesn't try to fool herself that she could
eat an entire big jackrabbit even if she were very hungry.
She doesn't hunt rabbits for food, but for sport. . .and for
the accolades her sporting spirit brings.

Once Kiki has "captured" one of these big bunnies, she
heads for home with her prize. Since these captives are too
big for her to carry or kill, she forces them to hop home.
Keeping her teeth on the rabbit's neck like a collar or chain,

she directs her hopping prisoner home for display. The two of them make their tedious half-hop, half-walk trek home so Kiki can show Lois, her owner, that she hasn't lost her edge.

Impossible? Not for this cat! Anyone who thinks a small cat can't corral a bigger, faster rabbit hasn't seen Kiki in action. And when she's been awarded with appreciative oohs, aahs, and "what have you got heres," Kiki releases her prisoner to hop his or her way back to safety—stretching a sore neck all the way.

Impossible is a word that is used little in the Bible. Possibly because "with God nothing shall be impossible," as the angel Gabriel told Mary (Luke 1:37 KJV). But its infrequent usage may make us all the more curious to investigate some of the contexts in which it is used.

Christ had to come to take away our sins because "it is impossible for the blood of bulls and goats to take away sins" (Hebrews 10:4). The sacrifices of the Old Testament were pointing to the ultimate sacrifice to come (10:8–14). Christ was triumphant in His sacrifice for our sins because "it was impossible for death to keep its hold on him" (Acts 2:24).

When it comes to problems that are bigger than we are, we need not fret. When the disciples asked Jesus why they were powerless to cast a demon out of a boy (which the Lord did with a simple rebuke), He told them, "If you have faith as small as a mustard seed. . .nothing will be impossible for you" (Matthew 17:14–21). In our own strength or by our own will many things are impossible, but Christ Himself assures us, "All things are possible with God" (Mark 10:24–27).

If you're facing an impossible task or situation today, take it to the One for whom nothing is impossible.

> If you're facing an impossible task or situation today, take it to the One for whom nothing is impossible.

Blackie

*A*s a single girl with no immediate prospects for a companion in the near future, Mary took a country kitten home with her from her sister's farm. She thought the personable black kitten would make a good companion. Perched like a bird on the passenger seat headrest, Blackie did well on the trip from Indiana to Illinois. But she was not well suited for apartment living. She had been used to wide-open spaces. Mary was seldom home. She had a full schedule with school, work, and piano lessons. They were not off to a good start.

One day a fellow piano teacher called Mary and asked if she could take on two more piano students. Mary thought for a moment and then gave her an answer.

"I'll trade you my cat for the two students."

The exchange was made. Mary had additional income from the added students, and her friend had a new pet that she loved and was home to enjoy. Over the years Blackie birthed a number of healthy litters. She was a delight to

Mary's friend and had a happy, productive life. Mary's friend still has a grandkitten of Blackie's.

Mary didn't fare as well on the exchange. The two piano students didn't last as long as it took Blackie to have her first litter of kittens.

God speaks of exchanges in the Bible. In the text above from 2 Corinthians, Paul begged his spiritual children to requite his love for them. "We are not withholding our affection from you, but you are withholding yours from us" (6:12). Paul felt shortchanged in his exchange of honest, open love.

God's indictment against people who turn their backs on Him is that they "exchanged the glory of the immortal God for images made to look like a mortal human being and birds and animals and reptiles" (Romans 1:23). As a result, "God gave them over. . .for the degrading of their bodies with one another" (verse 24). When people "exchanged the truth about God for a lie, and worshiped and served created things rather than the Creator" (verse 25), "God gave them over to shameful lusts" (verse 26). When "natural relations" are exchanged for "unnatural" ones, people will receive "in themselves the due penalty for their error" (verses 26–27). Unwise, unholy exchanges produce disastrous results.

Christ asked a poignant question: "What can anyone give in exchange for their soul?" (Matthew 16:26). In the context of His question, it is clear that to exchange one's soul for earthly gain or self-indulgence is to forfeit ourselves. To forfeit—or exchange—our souls leaves us utterly destitute.

> **The only way to avoid an exchange that will cost us everything is to follow Christ.**

The only way to avoid an exchange that will cost us everything is to follow Christ. Denying oneself—rather than indulging oneself—is the Lord's way (Mark 8:34). Only in losing our life for Christ's sake and that of the Gospel will we save it (verse 35).

What a beautiful exchange. . .a life dedicated to God in exchange for an eternity with God.

Peter

*D*riving down the four-lane highway, I almost missed the sight. Three little kittens, the mother cat, and a little girl were out in the front yard. The mother cat was bouncing along at a good clip. Two of her kittens were in precision pursuit, bouncing along directly behind her. Pursuing their mother vigilantly, these two were oblivious to everything around them. They didn't want Mom lost to their sight. But kitten number three, whom I nicknamed Peter, was not following after his mother.

Peter's attention was riveted on the little girl in front of him. She had turned to face him, and he was eagerly running to catch up with her. His siblings and mother cat were all but forgotten. They were headed one way; he was going in the opposite direction. Peter only had eyes for the blond-haired little girl before him. It was to her beckoning smile and extended arms he ran, hopping over and through the grass that was almost as tall as he was.

Unlike his siblings, Peter wanted the attentions and touch of another.

It was clear whom fuzzy little Peter had chosen to follow.

Whenever Jesus called anyone to Himself, or someone said they wanted to be closely allied with Him, Jesus simply said, "Follow me" (Matthew 4:19; 9:9; 19:21). Lest there be any doubt about how all-consuming following after Him is, the Lord said everything else takes second place. One man said to Christ, " 'Lord, first let me go and bury my father.' But Jesus told him, 'Follow me, and let the dead bury their own dead' " (8:21–22). Our allegiance to Christ Jesus takes precedence over all. Following Him cannot be taken lightly.

Jon and Jessie live in Guinea as missionaries. When one of the local Muslim women became a follower of Jesus Christ, she was thrown out of her home. This woman paid a price for being a Christ follower. After living with Jon and Jessie for several months, she was eventually able to secure a job and share an apartment with another woman. But her "family" no longer includes those related to her by blood. Following after Christ cost her all she'd had in the world.

Our command is: "Ever follow that which is good" (1 Thessalonians 5:15 KJV). If we are in positions of leadership, we are instructed to "offer ourselves as a model for [others] to imitate" (2 Thessalonians 3:9). The Lord said, "Whoever serves me must follow me" (John 12:26). We are not to follow "the ways of this world" (Ephesians 2:2), but Him who is "the way and the truth and the life" (John 14:6).

> The question remains: What and whom will we choose to follow?

"We did not follow cleverly devised stories when we told you about the coming of our Lord Jesus Christ in power," Peter wrote, "but we were eyewitnesses of his majesty" (2 Peter 1:16). There are myriad paths to follow; there are numerous leaders to follow. The question remains: What and whom will we choose to follow?

KitKat

God sets the lonely in families.
PSALM 68:6

*D*ashing across driveway and lawn, KitKat came running and meowing to greet Kelly daily. He was a scruffy stray (his name is short for kitty cat) who knew an easy mark when he saw one. Kelly would sit on the porch and talk to him. She didn't need or want another pet, but she had a soft spot for this adoring stray. So she left food out for him regularly, and he in turn repaid her generosity with uneaten portions of his other meals. But Kelly never invited him in.

One evening KitKat did not come up meowing and running. He could not even walk a straight line. Kelly found his head swollen, his nose running like a faucet, and his eyes rolling back in his head. She called an emergency veterinary number and was told to bring KitKat in immediately. Forty-eight hours (and considerably more dollars than that) later, Kelly brought the no-longer-a-homeless-stray-cat into her home to nurse him through the infection left behind by the other animal KitKat had battled.

Now Kelly has two tolerant dogs and two very pampered cats.

KitKat has a home and family.

Sandi and her husband wanted children. No amount of procedures or tests worked to help Sandi conceive. After several years of marriage, they finally resigned themselves to never having children—until Alex came along. . .and then Jordan. . .and finally Aaron. Sandi had not one, but three children. God "settles the childless woman in her home as a happy mother of children" (Psalm 113:9).

Other couples are not so blessed. But God gives them a promise of family, too. "Sing, barren woman, you who never bore a child; burst into song, shout for joy, you who were never in labor; because more are the children of the desolate woman than of her who has a husband" (Isaiah 54:1). In context this promise is to Israel, but God promises fulfillment to those who, though childless, are His. "And let no eunuch complain, 'I am only a dry tree.' For this is what the LORD says. . .'To them I will give within my temple and its walls a memorial and a name better than sons and daughters. . .' " (56:3–5).

Paul the apostle did not begrudge God his lack of a mate but saw his singleness as a way to wholly dedicate his life to God (1 Corinthians 7:7, 32–35). He also saw that God had given him a son in his beloved disciple Timothy (1 Timothy 1:2).

God may set us in the home as a happy mother of

children. He may not. Like KitKat, we may find ourselves with a family with whom we share no blood kinship. Our family may be those of our church family. Or our family may await us after we leave this life. Whatever the case, God "sets the lonely in families" (Psalm 68:6). For "the one who makes people holy and those who are made holy are of the same family. So Jesus is not ashamed to call them brothers and sisters" (Hebrews 2:11).

> Whatever the case, God "sets the lonely in families" (Psalm 68:6).

Princess Priscilla

He hath said in his heart, I shall not be moved.

PSALM 10:6 KJV

Priscilla was an abandoned stray that Becky's father brought home to her. A speckled gray cat who liked doing things her way, Priscilla was both mother cat several times over and superior hunter. One litter of kittens she decided to birth above the ceiling of the house over the furnace. It was no small feat for someone to climb up there and drag the kittens out one by one before they fell out of their precariously perched birthing bed.

What distinguished Priscilla as a princess was how she was "boss" around the barnyard. Becky's family had some big bird dogs, but they never troubled the princess. She was in charge, and that's the way it was, paws down.

When Becky and her mother had to move, Princess Priscilla again had her way. She did not want to leave the comfy coziness of the place she called home. She was free to roam and had lots of space. The dogs never bothered her, and it was a good place to raise a family. Priscilla was not moved with the rest of the family. The folks who bought the farm got a built-in mouser in the deal. Priscilla was no longer Becky's cat. The princess was unmovable.

The psalmist quoted the wicked man in the passage above as boasting in his invincibility. The New International Version translates this same verse as "Nothing will ever shake me" (Psalm 10:6). Although this man was not speaking of being literally moved from one dwelling to another like Priscilla, he was saying he couldn't be budged from his self-satisfied life. The psalmist describes such a man as arrogant, conniving, and haughty. He writes, "In all his thoughts there is no room for God" (verses 2–5).

Hopefully, we as Christians are not guilty of this kind of bravado. God may want to move us on occasion—out of our comfort zone, away from what is pleasantly familiar. God instructed Abram to move from Haran (Genesis 12:1–5). God moved the Israelites out of Egypt (Exodus 12:31–42). God has purposes for putting us where we find ourselves.

> God may want to move us on occasion—out of our comfort zone, away from what is pleasantly familiar.

In Acts we're told that God "marked out their [the nations'] appointed times in history and the boundaries of their lands" (Acts 17:26). The next verse supplies the reason for God's determination in this matter. "God did this so that they would seek him and perhaps reach out for him and find him, though he is not far from any one of us" (verse 27). God places us where we're most likely to seek Him.

How marvelously detailed is God's knowledge of each of us. Where we live, what we think (Psalm 94:11), the number of hairs on our heads (Luke 12:7)—it's all known to this One in whom "we live and move and have our being" (Acts 17:28).

Facing a move in your near future? "Do not move from the hope held out in the gospel" (Colossians 1:23). Rather, commit any and all of your "moves" to Him who "fills everything in every way" (Ephesians 1:23).

Sammy

*Therefore, holy brothers and sisters, who share in the heavenly
calling, fix your thoughts on Jesus, whom we acknowledge
as our apostle and high priest.*

HEBREWS 3:1

Sammy is a big-city cat. He and Esther, living in New York City, are like many New Yorkers. The two of them share a small apartment in a high-rise building. Not long ago Esther got up to go to work as she always did. She hustled out of the building and was just about to start her morning commute when she noticed everyone around her was looking up. Esther stopped to look up, too.

There, five stories up, on a window ledge hardly wider than his bottom, sat Sammy. Taking advantage of the early morning coolness, Sammy had stepped out of the open window for his morning bath. Totally oblivious to the staring, pointing crowd (and his very precarious position), Sammy methodically, slowly, and contentedly groomed himself.

Esther raced back into the building and up the stairs. Breathless, she opened her apartment door and went back in. Afraid she would startle Sammy into making an abrupt and fatal move, she called coaxingly to him.

"Here, Sammy! Come here, boy. I've got a treat for you!" She tried to keep her voice calm and musical although she was still puffing and panting from her dash up the steps. "Come on, buddy. Come on."

Sammy looked at her disinterestedly, but his tongue stopped. The smallest tip of it still stuck out of his mouth.

Hmm. Might as well see what she wants. . . .

Sammy moseyed back in without a look back. Esther slammed the window shut and never again has left a window up without a screen in.

"He's so heavenly minded he's no earthly good."

This tongue-in-cheek expression makes us smile but is really a contradiction in terms. Those who are heavenly minded are those who, because of their perspective, have the most to give. Their perspective, centered on the "man [from] heaven" (see 1 Corinthians 15:47), will be like His: focused on men and women of planet Earth. Unlike Sammy, they are not oblivious to those around them.

Paul said, "Since, then, we know what it is to fear the Lord, we try to persuade others" (2 Corinthians 5:11). The writer of Hebrews commended his fellow believers who were under persecution. They endured their suffering— and ministered to those undergoing similar suffering— knowing they had "better and lasting possessions" (Hebrews 10:34) beyond the here and now. When the Lord's disciples were looking heavenward as Jesus returned to His Father, they were asked, "Why do you stand here looking into the sky?" (Acts 1:11). The command had been given (verses 4, 8); it was time to get to work. When our minds are fixed on Jesus, our lifestyle will be one of service to others.

> **When our minds are fixed on Jesus, our lifestyle will be one of service to others.**

Today as you leave your time of prayer, your intimate place of communion with Him who fills heaven and earth, be ready to be faithful to your "heavenly calling." You may have to rescue someone from an unheavenly precipice of self-absorption.

DJ

*Yet when I surveyed all that my hands had done
and what I had toiled to achieve, everything was meaningless,
a chasing after the wind.*

ECCLESIASTES 2:11

It turned out to be one of those Sunday mornings.

Trudy had gotten herself and her two young daughters, Kendra and Karli, ready for church. Her husband was out of town on business, so it was just the three of them. Trudy was mentally patting herself on the back. They were even on time! Then it happened.

Karli had set DJ's cat food out on the back porch. DJ began eating. All of a sudden, a big, black stray cat jumped up onto the porch. The fur went up, the ears went back, and the threatening growls escalated to a screeching, hissing, biting tumble down the steps! Karli screamed for help and bolted out the door. DJ took off, scrambling away from the aggressor.

"DJ! DJ will be killed!"

Kendra ran out screaming. She dashed around the opposite side of the house to intercept and save DJ.

Trudy ran out, doing some screaming of her own.

"Stay away from the street! Don't run into the street!" Which daughter should she go after first?

Dust, dirt, cat spittle, and tearful screams had split the Sunday morning silence.

Karli pursued their cat, crying for poor DJ, who would be killed for sure.

Kendra rounded the house from the other side.

DJ dove under a bush.

Big Black never saw him and ran right by him—across the road and away.

Sobbing with relief, Karli picked up DJ. Clutching him to them, she and her sister carried him back to the house.

After dirtball DJ was safely rescued, Trudy looked at her weary daughters. Spent and wet with perspiration, all three sat breathing heavily. The girls' faces were puffy from crying and streaked with dirt. Their Sunday clothes were filthy—and full of cat hair. Trudy was in little better shape herself.

And—no surprise—they were going to be late for church.

As he aged, King Solomon looked back and was weary with what he saw. His wisdom and fame drew people from the world over. His building programs were second to none, his wealth unrivaled (1 Kings 3–7; 9–10). But his repeated phrase in Ecclesiastes is "meaningless, a chasing after the wind." (See Ecclesiastes 1:14, 17; 2:11, 17, 26; 4:4, 6, 16; 6:9.) The Lord said to His people who were preoccupied with everything but Him, "You have not wearied yourselves for me" (Isaiah 43:22).

Do we weary ourselves for God?

Do we weary ourselves for God? When the Israelites brought animals for sacrifice that did not meet God's standard, their excuse was, "What a burden!" (Malachi 1:13). They found obedience wearisome. But God was incensed. " 'Cursed is the cheat who has an acceptable male in his flock. . .but then sacrifices a blemished animal to the Lord. For I am a great king,' says the LORD Almighty" (verse 14).

We must be careful not to "weary [ourselves] with sinning" (Jeremiah 9:5). Rather, let us apply ourselves to wearying ourselves in pursuit of our God. He is worthy of honor and worship to the point of weariness.

Beyond the Hard Knocks. . .
the Hard Questions. . .
the Hard Times

*A little drowsy cat is an image
of perfect beatitude.*

JULES CHAMPFLEURY

Caleb

Even when I am old and gray, do not forsake me, my God,
till I declare your power to the next generation,
your mighty acts to all who are to come.

Caleb is an elderly orange cat. He seldom goes outside, which used to be his daily summertime practice. With one exception, Caleb the curmudgeon doesn't like the rest of the household cats. He's a little more tolerant of his owner, Jean, but he hisses at her occasionally, too.

Now that he is old, Caleb has developed a very annoying habit. He sprays—in the house. Jean says that others probably would have tossed him long ago, but she chooses to keep him.

In spite of Caleb's sour disposition and the necessity of protecting her walls and carpet as best as she can, Jean still loves and cares for him. Caleb may be old, and he may be cantankerous, but Jean is determined that he end his days where he began them—surrounded by her unconditional love.

As I age, the psalmist's prayer in Psalm 71 becomes ever

more special. Listen to the heart of this old saint: "You have been my hope, Sovereign LORD, my confidence since my youth. . . . I have become a sign to many; you are my strong refuge. . . . Do not cast me away when I am old; do not forsake me when my strength is gone" (verses 5, 7, 9).

As the great prophet Samuel neared the end of his earthly life, he never diminished in spiritual stature before God or the people of Israel. In his prime he was a man of integrity, held in high esteem among his people (1 Samuel 3:19–20). As an elderly man, Samuel commanded respect because of his godly character and his power with God. "Samuel called on the LORD, and that same day the LORD sent thunder and rain. So all the people stood in awe of the LORD *and of Samuel*" (12:18, emphasis added).

> As the great prophet Samuel neared the end of his earthly life, he never diminished in spiritual stature before God or the people of Israel.

Feeling old today? Be like the psalmist who said, "My mouth will tell of your righteous deeds, of your saving acts all day long—though I know not how to relate them all" (Psalm 71:15). Even at the end of his full life, that elderly songwriter was hard pressed to speak adequately of the righteousness and salvation of God Almighty.

Maybe you're on the far side of eighty and feel you have nothing to contribute—or that, if you do, no one wants to hear it anyway. Emulate Samuel. "As for me," he said, "far be it from me that I should sin against the Lord by failing to pray for you" (1 Samuel 12:23). If he could do nothing else, Samuel could—and would—pray.

Samuel's prayers and ours are not of despair but hope. As the aging psalmist sang in a voice that quavered with age but rang with assurance: "Though you have made me see troubles, many and bitter, you will restore my life again" (Psalm 71:20).

Sheba

I will wait for the LORD.

ISAIAH 8:17

MacKenzie walked to her school every morning. Every morning Sheba followed her, trotting behind MacKenzie and her friends. When MacKenzie entered the building, Sheba had to remain outdoors. She then found her way around the building to MacKenzie's classroom and stared woefully through the window. The school windows back then had no shades or blinds, so Sheba proved to be no small distraction to the room full of children.

MacKenzie's mother went to answer her telephone. It was MacKenzie's teacher. "Come and get your cat, please."

Sheba was ready to wait all day, if need be, for MacKenzie.

Then one day, Sheba disappeared. MacKenzie and her siblings were heartbroken. MacKenzie especially sobbed and sobbed for her missing cat. Finally, after supper, her father confessed to his crimes—both of them. Sheba had not run away like he suggested. He had taken her away. Begrudgingly, but ashamed of his lie and what he had done, he took his weeping daughter in the car to where he had taken the long-haired cat.

After being left near a farm way out in the country, there was Sheba. Although it was hours later, Sheba had not moved from the spot. She had sat by her box, patiently waiting for MacKenzie.

Few of us like to wait. We don't like to wait in traffic. We hate waiting in line at the grocery store. Our time is as valuable as our doctor's, in whose office we often sit waiting in "the waiting room." (We even hate that term.) Waiting on God, or waiting for Him to answer, is not on our list of favorite things, either.

A precious, true story of a man who both waited on God and waited for God to answer his prayer is nestled in the book of Luke between the shepherds in the fields and scholars in the temple. Simeon "was righteous and devout. He was waiting for the consolation of Israel, and the Holy Spirit was on him" (Luke 2:25). Unlike the prophet Anna, Simeon did not stay at the temple day and night (verses 36–37). When Mary and Joseph brought Jesus to dedicate Him to God, Simeon was "moved by the Spirit" and "went into the temple courts" (verse 27).

Can you picture his joy as he took the infant Christ in his arms and blessed Him? Do you see tears streaming down his weathered face as he "praised God, saying: 'Sovereign Lord, as you have promised, you may now dismiss your servant in peace. For my eyes have seen your salvation' " (verses 28–30)? Simeon had waited; God had delivered.

Feeling today like you're in God's waiting room? "In repentance and rest is your salvation, in quietness and trust is your strength," we're reminded (Isaiah 30:15). "Blessed are all who wait for him!" exclaims Isaiah (verse 18). The man who awaited Christ's first coming was rewarded. We shall be, too. Christ will "appear a second time, not to bear sin, but to bring salvation to those who are waiting for him" (Hebrews 9:28).

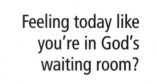

Feeling today like you're in God's waiting room?

Charlie

*"Why are you weeping and breaking my heart?
I am ready not only to be bound, but also to die in Jerusalem
for the name of the Lord Jesus."*

ACTS 21:13

Charlie, with blue eyes and snow-white fur and as loyal as a basset hound, loves his owner dearly. Whenever Betty is sick, he is by her side day and night. When she's had surgery, he never leaves her side. If Betty is feeling blue, all she says is, "Sing for me, Charlie," and her long-haired, sweet-natured cat purrs her to quietude.

Betty recently underwent knee replacement surgery. When she finally arrived home, Charlie would not leave her side except for his own "activities of daily living," as they're called in the health care industry. He proved himself once again to be a constant, loyal friend. But then the time came for Betty to begin her physical therapy.

Charlie did not appreciate the strangers who came to the house to help Betty with walking. Charlie kept getting underfoot (quite literally), frustrating the physical therapist, Betty, and her husband, who watched the proceedings. It didn't take but one or two visits from the therapist, and Charlie had to be confined to another room until therapy was completed.

Betty's "little white angel" meant well, but these times were for ambulating—not affection.

Compelled by the Spirit of God, Paul the apostle was determined to go to Jerusalem (Acts 20:22). Nonetheless, his loving, well-meaning friends tried to persuade him otherwise. Their pleadings didn't make his task any easier and only caused him grief.

Peter made the same mistake with the Lord Jesus. Smothering Him with his devotion, Peter tried to dissuade Christ from what He came to do. Peter's well-intentioned rebuke earned him an even harsher rebuke. "You do not have in mind the concerns of God," the Lord told him, "but merely human concerns" (Mark 8:31–33).

Mary Magdalene, overjoyed to see her Lord alive after His crucifixion, was reticent to let go of Him once He was within touching distance again. But the time had come for her to release Him. "Do not hold on to me," the Lord instructed her, "for I have not yet ascended to the Father. Go instead to my brothers" (John 20:16–17). In spite of His love for Mary, and her undying devotion to Him, the time had come for "letting go."

You may be in the midst of a painful letting-go process right now. You've done all you can to please and keep your spouse. Yet he still insists on leaving. Your grown child does not want to pursue the profession you felt fit her to a T.

Your best friend quits a secure, good-paying job to assume a pastorate in a struggling, little country church.

> Sometimes the clinging ends in a prayerful clasping of our hands.

Like Charlie, sometimes we must be put behind a closed door, separated from the one we love so he or she can take the next step—for good or ill—alone. Sometimes the clinging ends in a prayerful clasping of our hands.

Tiger

Even my close friend, someone I trusted,
one who shared my bread, has turned against me.

PSALM 41:9

Seven-year-old Megan has a cat by the name of Tiger. Tiger is aptly named. His personality and coloring are what you would expect when you visualize this domestic cat's cousin, the Bengal tiger. Megan loves her cat, but Tiger isn't quite the friend to Megan that she is to him. As soon as Megan lets down her guard, her cat is there to take advantage of her.

When Megan flops down on the sofa to read a book or watch television, Tiger will creep up to where her feet dangle enticingly over the edge of the couch. In a split second he jumps up, bites her toes, and darts off before Megan's surprised screech has echoed through the house. When it's time to eat, however, Tiger shows up all purrs and persuasive mews. He's innocence itself with whiskers and a tail.

Tiger's most despicable attack occurred at Megan's most vulnerable moment. Megan was just readying herself for bed. She did not know Tiger was behind her. She dropped her pants to pull on her pajama bottoms and—*sprinnng!*—in one lightning-quick move Tiger leaped up, bit her on the bottom, and darted out the door. Megan let out a scream, but it was too late. Her best buddy and furry foe—rolled into one ornery cat—had shot down the stairway, out of sight.

Both Megan and Tiger have an experiential understanding (from very different perspectives) of the old adage "biting the hand that feeds you."

We can laugh at a cat who has a peculiar way of demonstrating his devotion, but it's no laughing matter when a friend betrays us. Whether it's a betrayal of confidence or of loyalty, there's no disappointment like a friendship violated. David said, "If an enemy were insulting me, I could endure it. . . . But it is you, a man like myself, my companion, my close friend" who brought him pain (Psalm 55:12–13). The words he uses to express his distress resound with sorrow. He is "distraught" (verse 2); he is "in anguish" (verse 4).

The Lord Jesus Christ knows what it is like to have a friendship violated. When Jesus told His disciples that He knew one of them would betray Him, the Word says He was "troubled in spirit" (John 13:21). The word picture is that of agitation of water in a pool. The Lord knew what was coming, and by whom it was coming, but that didn't make it any easier. He was troubled, disquieted, agitated. The betrayal of a friend is painfully upsetting.

Where can we turn when a friend betrays us? Like David, in times of betrayal we can turn to our Lord, who knows firsthand how it feels to be betrayed by a close friend (Psalm 55:16–17). Jesus' friendship is for keeps. He proved it by His death (John 15:13). He is the "friend [who] loves at all times" (Proverbs 17:17), the "friend who sticks closer than a brother" (18:24).

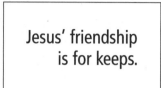

Jesus' friendship is for keeps.

Varmint

Then people go to their eternal home.

ECCLESIASTES 12:5

Varmint was not happy with his home. Thin, weathered, and looking the loser after one fight too many, he wandered into Karen's yard late one night. Karen took him in and learned, at least in part, the reason for Varmint's sorry condition. He was a declawed cat who had been loose in a world of clawed animals.

Why would anyone go to the trouble of declawing a cat and then put him outside? she wondered. *Maybe he got out by accident. . . .*

Putting her concerns aside, Karen did what she thought she ought to do after caring for the wanderer she named "Varmint." She put up signs around town and waited for someone to call and claim the sweet-natured obsidian black cat. Admittedly, she was glad when no one called. With no response, Karen took Varmint to the vet and got him a necessary "once-over" and vaccinations. But some weeks later, she got a telephone call.

"I saw a sign some time ago. I think you might have my cat."

Sure enough, Varmint was really Salem, the stranger's long-lost kitty. Appreciative of Karen's TLC for Salem/Varmint, the woman reimbursed her for the veterinary bills and left, taking her cat with her. Karen was sure she'd seen the last of Varmint.

A few weeks later, there sat Varmint on Karen's doorstep.

Home for most of us is the one place we want to be. It is the haven that beckons to us. Sometimes our home is neither of those. So we go about establishing a new one that is all those things ours never was.

> Home for most of us is the one place we want to be. It is the haven that beckons to us.

As Christians we often lose sight of the reality that where we are now—here on planet Earth—is not the consummate home God has in mind for us. Peter calls us "foreigners and exiles" in the world (1 Peter 2:11). "Foreigners" refers to sojourners who are temporary dwellers—people who do not have an established habitation in the place where they presently live. "Exiles" are foreigners who have settled "next to or among the native people." Although this world is all we have ever known, God tells us it is not our home. Even the bodies we live in are referred to as temporary dwellings (2 Peter 1:13–14). The Lord is busy preparing a home for us so we can be where He is (John 14:2–3).

Neda is elderly and dying of cancer. Mark is middle aged and healthy. Both of them love the Lord Jesus Christ and are eager to "go home." Both look forward to putting off the mortal and putting on the immortal (1 Corinthians 15:54). They well know that—wonder of wonders!—God Himself is our dwelling place (Psalm 90:1).

Karen did not remember Varmint's first owner's name or address. But clearly Varmint was more content to be back where he longed to be, even if it wasn't where he belonged. Varmint recognized "home," and he bravely fought and found his way back.

For Neda and Mark, it's expectantly looking forward to being "home with the Lord" (2 Corinthians 5:8).

Trouble

"As a mother comforts her child, so will I comfort you."
Isaiah 66:13

Trouble was not even three weeks old when he came into Cindy's life. He was not yet weaned and had been left motherless. The totally black kitten came to Cindy during a bleak and black time for her own soul. Depressed and alone, Cindy welcomed the small feline into her life.

An unweaned kitten demands time and attention—and patience. At this time in her life, Cindy had all those things to give to Trouble. She fed him by hand, cleaned up after him, and let him snuggle under her chin to sleep. Their relationship was a mutually dependent one for a while, but Trouble—by his very need of her—helped Cindy through her dark days. With Cindy's tender care, Trouble grew to a mature cat.

Those dark days have passed for both Trouble and Cindy. Cindy now has a husband and children; Trouble has two other cats and a dog with which to deal. But nine years later the pattern remains. Trouble curls up under Cindy's chin for those long hours of sleep.

He well remembers his source of comfort.

Whether He sends the comfort in the form of a friend, a pet, or the Holy Spirit, God the Father is "the Father of compassion and the God of all comfort" (2 Corinthians 1:3). Sometimes God's methods or sources of comfort come from unexpected quarters.

Naomi had left Bethlehem with her husband and sons to live in Moab. Anguish followed anguish, however. First, Naomi's husband died. Then her two sons died. Bereft, Naomi returned to her hometown of Bethlehem.

> **Sometimes God's methods or sources of comfort come from unexpected quarters.**

One of her daughters-in-law stayed in Moab, but her other Moabite daughter-in-law refused to leave her. Naomi had the devotion and comfort of this young woman from another culture and country (Ruth 1).

Now it was young Ruth's turn to be in a strange land as a widow. Yet she, too, found help from an unlikely source. The man whose fields she gleaned made sure she was protected although she was alone. He praised her for her loyalty to her mother-in-law and spoke a blessing over her. Ruth's response was in keeping with her humility: "May I continue to find favor in your eyes, my lord. . . . You have put me at ease by speaking kindly to your servant" (Ruth 2:8–13).

From days of trouble and sorrow, God eventually brought great joy. Boaz, the man who protected the young widow Ruth, became her kinsman-redeemer and her husband. Naomi's friends told her, "Your daughter-in-law, who loves you. . .is better to you than seven sons" (4:9–15). Naomi dandled Ruth's baby boy on her knee. Ruth became the great-grandmother of King David (4:13–22).

Is today one of your bleak days? Has the "bottom fallen out"? The Lord is neither unaware of nor indifferent to your need of help or comfort. "Indeed, he who watches over Israel will neither slumber nor sleep" (Psalm 121:4). Anticipate an unlikely source of comfort.

It may come from the God of all comfort "on little cat feet."

Saige

Why, LORD, do you stand far off?
Why do you hide yourself in times of trouble?

PSALM 10:1

They were gone. All five of them.

Roger had looked in every corner, behind every bale of straw, and under every box in their barn for Saige's new litter of kittens. For some unknown reason, Saige had moved her kittens from their safe spot in the barn. There was no pleasant mewing echoing in the barn. When the weather suddenly turned cold, Roger decided the poor kittens must have frozen to death out in the elements.

Some time later, Saige came across the yard with one of her kittens trotting merrily behind her! Roger and his family renewed their search. Finally, in the little-used family van, three more kittens were found safe and sound. The kittens had never left the barn; the van was parked inside it. Saige had simply moved her babies to a place she deemed safer and warmer.

Try as he might, however, neither Roger nor anyone else could find the fifth kitten. He looked in the engine, crawled under the chassis, and pulled up seats, but the fifth kitten was not to be found—and not one weak mew was heard.

Sometimes we have searched for the Lord in time of need only to find He is hidden from us. Job cried out to God, who seemed to be in hiding. "Why do you hide your face?" he asked (Job 13:24). Job, according to God's own estimate of him, was "blameless and upright" (1:8). Yet Job lost everything: his children, his wealth, and his health (1:13–22; 2:1–8). To lose all, and then be bereft of God, too. . .little wonder Job "cursed the day of his birth" (3:1).

We think of Psalms as the biblical book of praise, yet it, too, is sprinkled liberally with cries to the hidden God. "How long will you hide your face from me?" David asked (Psalm 13:1). Heman, the writer of Psalm 88, was not feeling like a "he-man." "Why, LORD, do you reject me and hide your face from me?" (verse 14). Why does God hide when we need Him the most?

As often as people cry out to God who seems to hide from them, God assures us He is always with us. After three years of speaking with Him face-to-face, the disciples could no longer touch the flesh of Jesus or hear His laughter or see Him smile. Yet Jesus said, "I am with

> As often as people cry out to God who seems to hide from them, God assures us He is always with us.

you always" (Matthew 28:20). He is Immanuel, God with us (1:23).

Later in Psalm 10 the psalmist does an about-face. He does not ask why God hides Himself in times of trouble. He says, "But you, God, see the trouble of the afflicted; you consider their grief and take it in hand" (verse 14). Not only is God not hidden, but He is in a position to do something about our troubles!

Hours from home, Roger was driving the van. Suddenly, there was kitten number five, climbing up beside him, mewing for its mother. Just like God, the kitten was there all the time.

Rachel

$\mathcal{F}$or years the pattern was unchanged.

"Time to go to bed, Rachel," Katy would say.

The perfectly symmetrical calico cat with the raccoon face would go to the basement door. Katy would open it, and Rachel would go down to her bed for the night. In the morning Katy went to that same door. There Rachel would be standing, ready for a new day. Suddenly, sweet-tempered Rachel changed the pattern.

"Time to go to bed, Rachel," Katy announced.

Instead of going directly to the basement door, Rachel came over and jumped up on Katy's lap. She stared Katy in the face and received a few loving strokes. Then she went to the basement door.

"Now that was strange," Katy said to her husband and daughter as she opened the door for Rachel.

The next morning Katy opened the basement door as usual, but Rachel was not there. Katy's gentle cat had quietly died during the night.

Rachel's last lingering look had been her way of saying good-bye.

As she made sure she was comfortable for the night, the young woman asked her aunt, "How are you feeling?"

Although she was receiving end-of-life care for her cancer, Esther's eyes brightened in response. "Actually, I feel pretty good tonight!"

With a kiss and a switch of the light, Esther's niece left the room.

Later that night Esther left the room, too—to be with her Lord.

"The Lord said to Moses, 'Now the day of your death is near' " (Deuteronomy 31:14). Moses was then given a song for his people (31:19, 22, 30; 32:1–43). Before he died, Joshua said, "Now I am about to go the way of all the earth. You know. . .that not one of all the good promises the Lord your God gave you has failed" (Joshua 23:14). As Paul the apostle bid farewell to the Ephesian elders, what "grieved them most was his statement that they would never see his face again" (Acts 20:38).

Though painful, it is a blessing to be able to share a final farewell with dear ones. Many are not so fortunate. Adam and Eve surely never expected the premature death of their son Abel at the hand of his brother (Genesis 4:1–8). David's dearest friend, Jonathan, was killed in battle.

Their parting had been painful, but David probably did not suspect he would never see Jonathan again (1 Samuel 20:16–42; 2 Samuel 1:4–5, 11–12).

Surely one of God's reasons for admonishing us not to "let the sun go down while [we] are still angry" is to spare us unnecessary regret (Ephesians 4:26). We say "good-bye" and "see you later" dozens of times a day. It is to our benefit and the blessing of others that we part kindly and gently. We don't know what a day may bring. Let our routine, simple good-byes be "always full of grace" (Colossians 4:6).

> Let our routine, simple good-byes be "always full of grace" (Colossians 4:6).

Grace

The Spirit of the Sovereign LORD is on me. . .to bestow. . .
the oil of joy instead of mourning, and a garment
of praise instead of a spirit of despair.

ISAIAH 61:1, 3

*S*he was at the end of her rope.

Despair had wrapped its tentacles about her. Alison was a single woman living alone in Lebanon. As a Christian missionary, she had seen little response to her labor of love and sacrifice for the people in the city where she lived. Her life was at risk every day. Her family was oceans away. The other missionaries around her had their spouses. She had no one. Her prayers went seemingly unheard. She was sure she would die of despair or loneliness—or both—in a culture hostile to her and to her God.

At this, her lowest point, there was a noise at her door.

Alison went to the door. A small calico cat sat on her doorstep, mewing mournfully. Bedraggled beyond description, the kitten brought a smile to Alison's face. The cat looked to be in worse shape than she was! And whereas she had friends, this cat had none. She had a home to live in; the kitten had none. She had food in her refrigerator. The scrawny cat probably hadn't eaten in days. She had the Lord to call on in her misery. This mewing mop of besotted fur had only her.

Alison scooped up her Special Delivery gift in her arms. She named her Grace.

Surely Jeremiah the prophet felt like Alison. He was sent not to another culture, but to his own people without results. Jeremiah voiced his despondency to the Lord. "I have not run away from being your shepherd; you know I have not desired the day of despair" (Jeremiah 17:16). He was doing what God had called him to do, yet "the day of despair" had pursued him, hunted him, and now held him. Just as it did with Alison.

Unlike his contemporary counterpart, however, God did not send Jeremiah even so much as a homeless kitten to help him through the day of despair. No such "Grace" was forthcoming. Things went from bad to worse. Jeremiah went from the stocks to prison to exile (see Jeremiah 20:2; 32:2; 43:1–7).

When our despair is at its greatest, the Lord may send immediate grace. At other times He may choose to give us a promise for a better day. To Jeremiah and his unrepentant countrymen He said, "For I know the plans I have for you. . .plans to prosper you and

> **When our despair is at its greatest, the Lord may send immediate grace.**

not to harm you, plans to give you hope and a future. Then

you will call on me and come and pray to me, and I will listen to you. You will seek me and find me when you seek me with all your heart" (Jeremiah 29:11–13).

You may have to open the Bible to find the grace you need for today. You may have to open your front door. Either way, be ready to find grace that comes from "the God of all grace" (1 Peter 5:10).

Thomas

It was just before the Passover Festival.
Jesus knew that the hour had come for him
to leave this world and go to the Father.

JOHN 13:1

Thomas the tomcat was saved from the "mean streets." Gina found him as a little kitten abandoned and barely acknowledged by people who said he'd been "hanging around for about a month or so" yet took no time to feed or care for the stray. Gina took him home to her mother, Vi.

Thomas has shown little appreciation for Gina since she delivered him from a life of indifferent passersby, but he showers affection on Vi. But that's not to say Thomas hasn't come without a challenge.

Residents of Vi's apartment complex have easy access to emergency services. One pull on a cord immediately summons a guard who can then call the needed emergency personnel. More than once Thomas has taken it upon himself to summon help. Vi has tried over and over to keep the emergency cords out of Thomas's reach but within hers. But she's had to apologize more than once when Thomas has summoned security to her apartment.

One question yet remains. Will Thomas pull the cord if there ever is a real emergency?

A recurring phrase stands out in the Gospel of John. Jesus' "time had not yet come." In two of the passages, it is clear that the time spoken of is in reference to the Lord's death (John 7:30; 8:20). The Lord was confident in the Father's timing. He did not put God the Father to the test unnecessarily. He refused to let Satan goad Him into a theatrical lifesaving rescue (Luke 4:9–12); neither did He purposely put Himself in harm's way when discretion dictated a safer course (John 7:1–10). But always He was confidently cognizant of His Father's timetable.

We do not have knowledge as full as that of the Lord Jesus. To His brothers Jesus said, "My time is not yet here; for you any time will do" (John 7:6). This verse suggests that our death may be at any moment. We have no way of knowing. We don't possess the knowledge or foresight of the Lord. We don't know when (or even if) we'll need to pull an emergency cord. Yet we do not need to be afraid. He who made us knows the number of our days (Psalm 37:18). Not even the death of a sparrow is missed by the loving, watchful eye of our Father. "Are not two sparrows sold for a farthing?" the Lord asked. "And one of them shall not fall on the ground without your Father" (Matthew 10:29 KJV).

Whether the cat pulls the emergency cord when there

is no emergency, or we can't reach it when there is, God is not out of our reach. "Call on me in the day of trouble," God says. "I will deliver you, and you will honor me" (Psalm 50:15). When we stand before the Lord, we will know our times were always in His trustworthy hands (31:15).

> When we stand before the Lord, we will know our times were always in His trustworthy hands.

Misha

Even though I walk through the darkest valley,
I will fear no evil.

PSALM 23:4

Misha is terrified of children. As far as Karen, her owner, knows, Misha has never been tormented or abused by children, yet she is still frightened by them. Whether the child is a busy toddler or a teenager with a telephone wired to his head, Misha avoids children at all costs. This is very difficult for Misha for several reasons.

Problem number one: Karen has a toddler. Problem number two: Karen and her husband are group home parents for several delinquent and neglected teenage boys. Misha's residence is on the third floor with Karen and her own family. The boys' rooms are on the second floor. Problem number three: Misha's litter box is in the basement.

Even when Karen is home and all the boys are at school for the day, Misha does not like leaving the safety of her upper room. Karen says she can almost hear Misha's thoughts as she makes her timid, cautious, wary trek to the basement.

Even though I walk through the valley of the shadow of death. . .

In 1952 Grace and her husband were living in what was then called Borneo. In the summer a dose of worm medicine finally freed their toddler of a wriggling, ten-inch worm. In October Grace's husband, Bill—neither a nurse nor a physician—delivered his wife of their newest daughter. Surely at times Grace was convinced she was walking "through the valley of the shadow of death." Over and again, these missionaries saw God safely lead them through shadowed valleys.

The disciples must have felt like Grace and Misha as they left the upper room (Luke 22:12–39). After three years of relative peace and safety with their Lord, His marching instructions changed. "But now if you have a purse, take it, and also a bag; and if you don't have a sword, sell your cloak and buy one" (verse 36).

Each of us receives our own set of "orders" from the Lord. For some of us, it means early martyrdom, as it did for the apostle James (Acts 12:2). For others, it means serving as missionaries in lands fraught with peril. For some of us, it means caring for an ailing parent who no longer knows us. For others, it means spending the last twenty years of our long life without our "lifelong" mate.

Whatever our situation, like the author of Psalm 23, we can look to our Maker and confidently declare, "You are with me" (verse 4). Like Asaph of Psalm 77, someday we will look back and say to God, "Your path led through the sea, your way through the mighty waters, though your footprints were not seen" (verse 19).

> The unseen One whose radiance dispels every shadow is closer than breath.

Are you facing a walk through some dark shadows today? Like Grace, like the disciples of Jesus, like David, Asaph, and even like Misha, you are not alone. The unseen One whose radiance dispels every shadow is closer than breath.

Baxter and Rocky

It was about this time that King Herod arrested
some who belonged to the church,
intending to persecute them.
He had James, the brother of John,
put to death with the sword.

ACTS 12:1–2

*S*upercats Baxter and Rocky top the scales at twelve and fourteen pounds, respectively. These brother cats are as active and demanding as two young tomcats can be. Even if their food dish is full, they carry on in the morning until they are properly fed. That means their owner, Barb, has to go through the motions of filling their bowl with cat food even if it already has food in it. If their water dish is dry, they simply move the bowl to the middle of the room until Barb sees it—or steps on it—and refills it. Baxter is the lovable one of the two; Rocky is the bully. Generally these two siblings live in peaceful coexistence, but sometimes their vigorous play gets out of hand.

One day the two brothers were wildly tearing about the house. With their speed, all eight feet, and twenty-six-pound total weight, disaster was imminent. Sure enough,

Rocky and Baxter had a midair collision. Rocky kept going, no worse for the crash.

Baxter was knocked out cold.

Times and attitudes change. In the early days of the young Christian church, the Christians were "highly regarded by the people" (Acts 5:13). Less than fifteen years later, the apostle James was martyred (12:2). James's brother John lived a very long life. Both James and John enjoyed a special relationship with the Lord Jesus Christ. The two of them, along with Simon Peter, were the only eyewitnesses of Jesus' transfiguration (Matthew 17:1–3). Jesus had a nickname for the two brothers (Mark 3:17), and the two of them, again with Peter, were closest to the Lord as He prayed alone in Gethsemane (14:33). Although Peter, too, was martyred years before John died, he also lived a fairly long life. Of the three men, only James died young.

Why?

Why does a midair collision knock out one cat while the other walks away unharmed?

Why does God take one brother home to be with him at a young age and give the other a long life?

We can become overwrought trying to answer unanswerable questions. We can't know why a godly woman in perfect health, living in loving obedience to the Lord, is killed in an automobile accident. We can't understand why God gives long life to another obedient servant who now knows neither anything nor anyone as he languishes in the end stages of dementia. We cannot know or understand these things.

What can we know?

"He is the Rock, his works are perfect, and all his ways are just. A faithful God who does no wrong, upright and just is he" (Deuteronomy 32:4). "The LORD's unfailing love surrounds the one who trusts in him" (Psalm 32:10), and "he [the LORD] is faithful in all he does" (33:4).

> **We can't know or understand it all, but we can know the One who does.**

We can't know or understand it all, but we can know the One who does.

Marbles

*"But no one says, 'Where is God my Maker,
who gives songs in the night,
who teaches us more than he teaches the beasts
of the earth and makes us wiser than the birds in the sky?' "*

Job 35:10–11

Verdi's *Othello*.

Marbles is a discerning calico cat who loves opera music. She particularly likes Verdi; *Othello* is her personal favorite. When her owner, Barb, starts the CD playing and the notes of the opera fill the room, Marbles ceases whatever it is she's doing. The laser light is ignored, the food sits uneaten in the bowl, and even her companion, Smokey, is snubbed. (Smokey couldn't care less about *Othello* or any other opera.) Marbles comes out of her kitty condo and sits atop it. She throws her head back, her whiskered face a study in delight, and listens rapturously. Sometimes she purrs. Marbles is mesmerized as the notes transport her into ecstasy.

In Barb's words, Marbles is "blissed out."

Music. It is at its best when it comes from within us, when it first comes from God Himself. God gives songs in the night. He did it for Paul and Silas as they were in the stocks in a prison cell in Philippi (Acts 16:22–25). Paul and Silas had been stripped, beaten, and "severely flogged." There were no simple amenities in their cell. Their wounds were not attended to before they were chained. Yet they sang because they knew the One who "gives songs in the night."

> Music. It is at its best when it comes from within us, when it first comes from God Himself.

Years ago friends of ours had a teenage daughter who was dying of cancer. This was before the medical community was vigilant in pain management, before hospice or end-of-life care was liberal with pain control in the home setting. This couple awoke during the night, knowing their beautiful, bright, and only child was in constant pain. Pain they were unable to alleviate or control. They heard her crying out to God quietly in her suffering, praying to Him to help her. Heartsick with her quiet cries and soft weeping, they stood outside her room for a moment. Then they heard something else.

They heard her sing.

Quietly, gently, lovingly, their little girl started singing. Singing to the Lord Jesus Christ who would soon take her into His very arms. Singing to the One who gives songs in the night.

As discerning as Marbles is about good music, she knows nothing about these kinds of songs. Only to humankind has the Creator given the ability to sing in times of great suffering. Times during the soul's dark night. He "teaches more to us than to the beasts of the earth." He makes us wiser than myriad songbirds. Though this kind of song is beyond the understanding of God's beasts and birds, the Lord can teach us His night songs. "By day the Lord directs his love, at night his song is with me" (Psalm 42:8).

The Lord God alone gives songs when there's nothing earthly to sing about.

Bibliography

Jensen, Irving L. *Jensen's Survey of the Old Testament.* Chicago: Moody Press, 1978.

Pfeiffer, Charles F., and Everett F. Harrison, eds. *The Wycliffe Bible Commentary.* Chicago: Moody Press, 1962.

Scofield, C. I., ed. *Oxford NIV Scofield Study Bible.* New York: Oxford University Press, 1984.

Strong, James. *Strong's Exhaustive Concordance of the Bible.* Iowa Falls, IA: Riverside Book and Bible House.

Zodhiates, Spiros, ed. *The Complete Word Study Dictionary: New Testament.* Chattanooga: AMG Publishers, 1992.